# Samson

*This fountain in Russia depicts the story of Samson killing a lion, as described in Judges 14:5–6.*

## Money at its Best: Millionaires of the Bible

| | |
|---|---|
| Abraham and Sarah | Joseph |
| Daniel | Moses |
| David | Noah |
| Esther | Samson |
| Jacob | Solomon |
| Job | Wealth in Biblical Times |

MONEY *at its* BEST

# Samson

Denise-Renée Barberet

Mason Crest Publishers
Philadelphia

Produced by OTTN Publishing.
Cover design © 2009 TLC Graphics, www.TLCGraphics.com.

**Mason Crest Publishers**
370 Reed Road, Suite 302
Broomall PA 19008
www.masoncrest.com

Copyright © 2010 by Mason Crest Publishers. All rights reserved.
Printed and bound in the United States of America.

First printing

1 3 5 7 9 8 6 4 2

Library of Congress Cataloging-in-Publication Data

  Barberet, Denise-Renée.
   Samson / Denise-Renée Barberet.
       p. cm. — (Millionaires of the Bible)
   Includes bibliographical references.
   ISBN 978-1-4222-0475-7 (hardcover)
   ISBN 978-1-4222-0850-2 (pbk.)
  1.  Samson (Biblical judge)—Juvenile literature. 2.  Bible. O.T.—
Biography—Juvenile literature.  I. Title.
   BS580.S15B37 2008
   222'.32092—dc22
                                                                          2008046716

Publisher's Note: The Web sites listed in this book were active at the time of publication. The publisher is not responsible for Web sites that have changed their address or discontinued operation since the date of publication. The publisher reviews and updates the Web sites each time the book is reprinted.

# Table of Contents

| | |
|---|---:|
| Samson and His Wealth | 6 |
| Introduction: Wealth and Faith | 7 |
| 1. Samson the Nazirite | 11 |
| 2. Journey to the Promised Land | 18 |
| 3. The Philistines | 35 |
| 4. The Judges | 41 |
| 5. The Birth of Samson | 48 |
| 6. Samson's Revenge | 55 |
| 7. Samson Betrayed | 67 |
| 8. Samson: the Myth and the Man | 79 |
| Notes | 94 |
| Glossary | 98 |
| Further Reading | 101 |
| Internet Resources | 103 |
| Index | 107 |
| Illustration Credits | 111 |
| About the Author | 112 |

# Samson and His Wealth

- Samson was born into what today would be considered a middle-class family. The Bible says that when his parents spoke to the Angel of the Lord, they offered him a young goat and grain, as a burnt sacrifice. "Then Manoah took a young goat, together with the grain offering, and sacrificed it on a rock to the Lord" (Judges 13:19).

- The Angel of the Lord told Samson's mother "No razor may be used on his head, because the boy is to be a Nazirite, set apart to God from birth, and he will begin the deliverance of Israel from the hands of the Philistines" (Judges 13:5). As Samson grew up, he was blessed by God.

- Although Samson was a godly man, he often fell into temptation. As a Nazirite, he was supposed to marry within his faith; however, he fell in love with a Philistine woman. His parents were greatly disappointed, but the Lord guided Samson's path. God used Samson's marriage as His way to confront the Philistines (Judges 14:4).

- Samson served as a judge of Israel for twenty years. He joined the ranks of honored judges like Deborah, Barak, and Gideon (Judges 15:20).

- The story of Samson proves that even though Samson often strayed from God's ways, in the end, he was faithful to God's will. Through his death, Samson destroyed more Philistines than he had when he was alive. He truly began the deliverance of the Israelites from the hands of the Philistines, just as God had promised.

# Introduction: Wealth and Faith

Many people believe strongly that great personal wealth is incompatible with deep religious belief—that like oil and water, the two cannot be mixed. Christians, in particular, often feel this way, recollecting Jesus Christ's own teachings on wealth. "Do not store up for yourselves treasures on earth, where moth and rust destroy, and where thieves break in and steal," Jesus cautions during the Sermon on the Mount (Matthew 6:19). In Luke 18:25, he declares, "It is easier for a camel to go through the eye of a needle than for a rich man to enter the kingdom of God"—a sentiment repeated elsewhere in the Gospels.

Yet in Judeo-Christian culture there is a long-standing tradition of material wealth as the manifestation of God's blessing. This tradition is amply reflected in the books of the Hebrew Bible (or as Christians know them, the Old Testament). Genesis 13:2 says that the patriarch Abram (Abraham) "had become very wealthy in livestock and in silver and gold"; the Bible makes it clear that this prosperity is a gift from God. Other figures whose lives are chronicled in

Genesis—including Isaac, Jacob, Joseph, Noah, and Job—are described as both wealthy and righteous. The book of Deuteronomy expresses God's promise of prosperity for those who obey his commandments:

> If you fully obey the Lord your God and carefully follow all his commands I give you today, the Lord your God will set you high above all the nations on earth. . . . The Lord will grant you abundant prosperity—in the fruit of your womb, the young of your livestock and the crops of your ground—in the land he swore to your forefathers to give you. (Deuteronomy 28:1, 11)

A key requirement for this prosperity, however, is that God's blessings must be used to help others. Deuteronomy 15:10–11 says, "Give generously . . . and do so without a grudging heart; then because of this the Lord your God will bless you in all your work and in everything you put your hand to." The book of Proverbs—written during the time of Solomon, one of history's wealthiest rulers—similarly presents wealth as a desirable blessing that can be obtained through hard work, wisdom, and following God's laws. Proverbs 14:31 promises, "The faithless will be fully repaid for their ways, and the good man rewarded for his."

Numerous stories and folktales show the generosity of the patriarchs. According to Jewish legend, Job owned an inn at a crossroads, where he allowed travelers to eat and drink at no cost. When they offered to pay, he instead told them about God, explaining that he was simply a steward of the wealth that God had given to him and urging them to worship God, obey God's commands, and receive their own blessings. A story about Abraham says that when he moved his flocks from one field to another, he would muzzle the animals so that they would not graze on a neighbor's property.

After the death of Solomon, however, the kingdom of Israel

was divided and the people fell away from the commandments God had mandated. The later writings of the prophets, who are attempting to correct misbehavior, specifically address unethical acts committed to gain wealth. "You trample on the poor," complained the prophet Amos. "You oppress the righteous and take bribes and you deprive the poor of justice in the courts" (Amos 5:11, 12). The prophet Isaiah insists, "Learn to do right! Seek justice, encourage the oppressed. . . . If you are willing and obedient, you will eat the best from the land; but if you resist and rebel, you will be devoured by the sword" (Isaiah 1:17, 19–20).

Viewed in this light, the teachings of Jesus take on new meaning. Jesus does not condemn wealth; he condemns those who would allow the pursuit of wealth to come ahead of the proper relationship with God: "No one can serve two masters. . . . You cannot serve both God and money" (Matthew 6:24).

Today, nearly everyone living in the Western world could be considered materially wealthier than the people of the Bible, who had no running water or electricity, lived in tents, walked when traveling long distances, and wore clothing handmade from animal skins. But we also live in an age when tabloid newspapers and trashy television programs avidly follow the misadventures of spoiled and selfish millionaire athletes and entertainers. In the mainstream news outlets, it is common to read or hear reports of corporate greed and malfeasance, or of corrupt politicians enriching themselves at the expense of their constituents. Often, the responsibility of the wealthy to those members of the community who are not as successful seems to have been forgotten.

The purpose of the series MONEY AT ITS BEST: MILLIONAIRES OF THE BIBLE is to examine the lives of key figures from biblical history, showing how these people used their wealth or their powerful and privileged positions in order to make a difference in the lives of others.

Samson, a powerful Israelite warrior, was one of the people known as Judges who led the Israelites during the first generations after their arrival in Canaan. His exploits are recorded in chapters 13 through 16 of the biblical Book of Judges.

# SAMSON THE NAZIRITE

The Book of Judges in the Old Testament is a collection of stories about early Jewish military leaders. Eleven men, and one woman, are chronicled in the Book's twenty-one chapters, but one of the twelve stands out from all the rest—Samson, an adventurous, yet deeply flawed, larger-than-life hero.

To Bible readers, Samson is as well known as Noah, Abraham, Moses, and even Jesus Christ. He was the superman of his generation, celebrated for his "divine" extraordinary physical strength. More importantly, Samson was chosen by God, in the same way that God chose Abraham, whom Jews recognize as the founder of the Jewish nation.

Yet Samson is an enigma, his life story a study in contradictions. His childless parents were already advanced in age when the Angel of the Lord told his mother that she would give birth to a son, and that God intended for their son to be a Nazirite, which meant he was expected to abstain from drinking wine, going near a dead body, or cutting his hair. Samson was supposed to devote his life to God, separate himself from unbelievers and wrongdoers, and save Israel from foreign invaders, specifically Israel's hostile neighbors and chief adversaries, the Philistines.

Instead, when Samson grows up, he freely carouses with the Philistines, who may have been the boozers of their day—pottery unearthed by modern-day archaeologists in Philistine-controlled areas suggests that the Philistines enjoyed their beer and wine, and created plenty of vessels in which to store it.

After a failed marriage to a Philistine woman, Samson embarks on murderous rampages against the Philistines—at one point he arms himself with the jawbone of a donkey and kills a thousand Philistines. But because he could not control his own desires, especially when it came to women, his enemies successfully schemed a way to cut his long hair, a symbol of his vow to God. In the end, Samson will end up bound, blinded, and forced to grind grain like a woman in the Philistine prison of Gaza.

One woman in particular, Delilah, is indelibly linked to his name. "Samson's name has become a byword for incredible strength, just as the name of Delilah, the woman he loved, is a byword for betrayal," Rabbi Joseph Telushkin wrote in *Jewish Literacy: The Most Important Things to Know about the Jewish Religion, Its People and Its History*.

The saga of Samson has inspired poets, dramatists, songwriters, and even Hollywood movie directors. The 1949 Cecil B. DeMille film *Samson and Delilah* is one of the most popular Hollywood epics of all time. Likewise, dozens of masters of European Christian painting have immortalized Samson and Delilah, including the Dutch

*This 17th-century painting by the Italian artist Carlo Cignani depicts Delilah cutting the sleeping Samson's hair.*

painter Rembrandt, early Italian Renaissance painters Michelangelo and Andrea Mantegna, and the Flemish Baroque painter Peter Paul Rubens, just to name a few. In 1743, German-born composer George Frideric Handel composed the oratorio *Samson*. Camille Saint-Saëns wrote an opera, *Samson et Dalila*, between 1868 and 1877. The seventeenth-century English poet John Milton immortalized Samson and Delilah in the tragic poem *Samson Agonistes* (1671). Folk songs about the fated couple still entertain audiences today.

Many biblical scholars and historians consider the saga of Samson as nothing more than myth, a sensational folk legend. "The stories of Samson are early Israeli folklore in its purest form," according to John L. McKenzie, author of *The World of the Judges*. "In the days when parts of Israel were dominated by their powerful Philistine neighbors, the Israelites had little comfort except in relating the story of the village hero who in life and death was too much for the Philistines to handle."

*In John Milton's poem* Samson Agonistes, *Delilah gives a parting speech in which she explains her motivation for betraying Samson: "[I]n my country, where I most desire,/in Ecron, Gaza, Asdod, and in Gath/I shall be named among the famousest/of women, sung at solemn festivals,/living and dead recorded, who to save/her country from a fierce destroyer, chose/above the faith of the wedlock-bands, my tomb/with odours visited and annual flowers."*

## THE PHILISTINES

Whether Samson was a real person or a folk hero will no doubt remain highly debatable. Nevertheless, to understand the complexities and contradictions that characterized his life and tragic death, as recorded in the Bible, requires an understanding of the time and circumstances in which Samson lived.

During Samson's twenty-year rule as a judge, the Israelites found themselves engaged in major conflicts with their neighbors, the Philistines. Samson was born into the Hebrew tribe of Dan, and the Philistines forced the Danites to leave their homes in the foothills, on the coast, and migrate north.

The origins of the Philistines are obscure—the Egyptians described them as "Sea Peoples" from the region around the Aegean Sea. According to the Bible, they were ruling over Israel at the time of Samson's reign as a judge. The Philistines held a significant military advantage over Israel because, among other things, they were skilled metalworkers, and possessed iron weapons. According to the Bible, Israel does not have iron weapons until the time of King David, some two centuries after the arrival of the Philistines.

Samson's first recorded run-in with the Philistines occurs when he chooses a Philistine woman for his wife, over the objections of his parents. "Isn't there an acceptable woman among your relatives or among our people? Must you go to the uncircumcised Philistines to get a wife?" Samson's parents ask. But Samson says to his father, "Get her for me. She is the right one in my eyes!" (Judges 14:3). The marriage turns into a fiasco, and this sets off a series of conflicts between Samson and the Philistines, including an incident in which Samson burns the fields, vineyards, and olive groves of the Philistines;

later he kills a thousand Philistines in a place called Ramathlehi ("the hill of the jawbone").

The Philistines ultimately prevail; they capture Samson. But in retaliation, Samson destroys their sacred temple, killing three thousand Philistines at the same time. It is an act of suicide, however, because Samson commits the act at the expense of his own life.

## A QUESTIONABLE HERO

Samson's actions have led many interpreters and commentators on ancient Jewish history to question whether he is worthy of the title "hero."

"Although Jewish tradition regards Samson as both a judge and a prophet, he is unlike any other judge and prophet," according to Rabbi Telushkin:

> While the Judges lead the whole Jewish community, Samson always acts alone; whereas the prophets deliver messages from God, Samson leaves behind no prophetic words. . . .
>
> In the end, this Jewish Hercules is destroyed not because of superior Philistine might but, because of his lust and obsession for non-Jewish women. His first wife is a Philistine (the Bible suggests that this was God's will, Judges 14:4); after her death he sleeps with Philistine harlots, and finally he falls in love with Delilah.

Even with all of his faults and weaknesses, the Bible narrative says that God uses Samson for His own purposes. In fact, the first sentence of Chapter 13 of the Book of Judges opens with, "Again the Israelites did evil in the eyes of the Lord, so the Lord delivered them into the hands of the Philistines for forty years" (Judges 13:1).

For centuries, Bible interpreters, commentators, and historians have attached a long list of unfavorable labels to the character of Samson: wild man, trickster, cad and cheat, self-indulgent egotist, slave to his physical passions, and fool preoccupied by personal vendettas. Yet, in the book of Hebrews, in the New Testament of the Christian Bible, he is listed as a "hero of faith."

"Samson is a hero because he gave the enemies and oppressors of Israel a very bad time before they caught him," McKenzie explains. "He is not unlike Robin Hood as a popular figure. He can be compared to a more recent folk hero, Jesse James, who was actually a cold-blooded thief and murderer, but who was a hero to many of his neighbors and a glamorous figure in legend because he annoyed the villains who operated the banks and the railroad. As a popular hero Samson needs no explanations; as a charismatic hero he is hard to swallow."

# Journey to the Promised Land

In a sense, Samson's story does not begin with Samson. Instead, he is a link in a long chain that stretches back to Abraham, considered by Jews to be the patriarch of the Hebrew people. Abraham was born and raised in the ruined city of Ur in Mesopotamia, in the southern part of present-day Iraq. Ur was a seaport on the Persian Gulf, at the mouth of the Euphrates River, some twelve miles from the traditional site of the Garden of Eden.

Centuries before Samson's birth, God called Abraham to leave his father's house and his homeland in the Fertile Crescent to settle in a new land, Canaan. God chose Abraham because he rejected idolatry, and worshiped only Him. Ur was a hotbed of cult activity; according to Jewish tradition, even Abraham's father sold idols.

Abraham settled in Canaan around 1738 B.C.E. Today, this land corresponds roughly to present-day Israel/Palestine, including the West Bank, western Jordan,

Journey to the Promised Land

Samson was descended from Abraham, a man whom God promised would be the father of many nations. Abraham obeyed God, even when He demanded that Abraham sacrifice his son Isaac. Because of Abraham's faith and his willingness to follow God's commands, God permitted Abraham to sacrifice a ram in Isaac's place.

southern and coastal Syria and Lebanon, continuing up to the border of modern Turkey. Bounded to the west by the Mediterranean Sea, to the north by mountains, and to the east and south by desert, it is a relatively small geographic area, about 10,000 square miles, or the approximate size of Vermont. It was not Canaan's size, but rather its location that made it strategically important, both in ancient times and today. Geologically, this area forms a land bridge between the continents of Asia and Africa.

The Book of Genesis records that God's promise of land was reaffirmed to Abraham's descendants: Isaac, Jacob, Joseph, and Jacob's other sons.

## SLAVES IN EGYPT

Generations passed after the death of Abraham, and over time the Israelites faced many crises. Famine drove the

*The Israelites lived in Egypt for more than 400 years. For much of that time, they were used as slaves by the Egyptians, until God sent a leader to free them from their bondage.*

# The Documentary Hypothesis

According to a longstanding tradition among Christians and Jews, Moses is the author of the first five books in the Bible. However, contemporary scholars generally agree that the Bible is the work of four distinct authors or groups of authors who compiled and edited material from different locations and sources over a period of centuries.

During the late 19th century, a theory of biblical authorship called the Documentary Hypothesis was formulated. Over the years there have been numerous variations on this theory. In its simplest form, the Documentary Hypothesis says that the main blocks of stories in the books of Genesis and Exodus—including the story of Noah—are the oldest material. They are attributed to two anonymous authors, known as J and E. The initials come from the names for God that each author uses in the narrative—J for "Yahweh" (in German, "Jahweh") and E for "Elohim." Scholars believe these two sets of stories were written down between 950 and 800 B.C.E., although they probably existed in oral form much earlier than that.

Around 600 B.C.E., new material concerned with religious or legal matters—such as the covenant between God and Abraham in Genesis 17, along with genealogical information—was added. This material is believed to have been the work of a priest or group of priests, and is labeled P.

The first five books of the Bible (referred to by Jews as the Torah) were placed in their final form around 400 B.C.E. by a group of editors, who blended the J, E, and P strands together and added new material. The addition is labeled R, after the group of redactors who concentrated on reworking and polishing the text.

Over the past two centuries the Biblical text has been the subject of intense scholarly scrutiny. This theory offers an understanding of how the book of Genesis might have been composed. However, there are still numerous points of disagreement among scholars, and many of them may be impossible to ever resolve.

*The Italian artist Michelangelo carved this statue of Moses. The Biblical book of Exodus describes how God enabled Moses to lead the Israelites out of slavery. Once the Israelites had departed from Egypt, God gave His people the Ten Commandments (opposite), as well as hundreds of other laws and restrictions to follow as they moved into the Promised Land, Canaan.*

Israelites out of Canaan and into Egypt. There, they coexisted with the Egyptians for many generations. However, the political tide eventually turned, and the Egyptians enslaved the Israelites. The Israelites remained captives of the Egyptians until God sent a deliverer, Moses, to start them on their journey back to Canaan. This period of time is known in the Bible as the Exodus, and nearly six hundred years had passed between the time of Abraham and the time of Moses.

Moses led more than 600,000 people—the number given in the book of Exodus—hundreds of miles through extraordinarily harsh desert wilderness, many on foot, many loaded down with possessions, and with untold numbers of cattle, sheep, and other animals, all of whom must be fed and watered. The journey to the Promised Land took the Hebrews forty years—and not all reached their final destination. God allowed Moses to see the Promised Land from the top of a mountain, but even he was not allowed to cross over. That was left to a new,

younger generation, led by Joshua—Moses' trusted aide, and one of twelve spies that Moses sent on a mission to explore the land of Canaan. He was one of only two spies who gave a favorable report of the land. The others reported that the land could not be taken; among other things, they said Canaan was occupied by giants.

## The Geography of Canaan

Canaan was not vacant land when the Israelites arrived there. The area had been inhabited by various groups of people for thousands of years. The small kingdoms of Edom and Moab, for example, had settled in Canaan about a half a century before the Israelite invasion. And according to modern archaeology, Ammon, another small state, had surrounded its territory with a series of small fortresses. These particular groups were not large or powerful, but they had kings and organized forms of government.

Many of Israel's neighbors, if not most, were more advanced and prosperous than the Israelites, who after all had spent forty years wandering in the desert—and before the desert journey they had spent four hundred years in Egypt (or 430, according to another tradition).

"When the Hebrews and Israelites entered Canaan, they found there a highly developed and sophisticated society," writes Harry M. Orlinsky in *Ancient Israel*. "Indeed, the Canaanite civilization was so advanced that it nearly absorbed the desert invaders. There can be no doubt that the Israelites of Joshua and Judges were quite unable to match the material techniques of Canaan, at least until the period of Solomon in the tenth century."

Nevertheless, Canaan was the land the Israelites believed that God had promised them. The land can be divided into four distinct regions running the length of the

*This map of the region known as Palestine, from an 1870 atlas, shows how the region was divided among the Israelite tribes. In historical and biblical literature, Canaan is the ancient name for Palestine. The origin of the term Canaan is obscure. As a geographical designation, it was in use as early as the third millennium* B.C.E. *Biblical writers used "Canaanites" as a general description for inhabitants of ancient Palestine. However, the people were not ethnically or politically united as a single nation, though they shared similar cultures and language.*

country in north-south strips. These regions are further divided into east and west regions by a line of waters that figure prominently in both the Old and New Testaments: the Sea of Galilee to the north, the River Jordan which flows from its southern end, and finally the extraordinarily salty waters of the Dead Sea at the southernmost end. To the east of the river lie the highlands of the Transjordan, often occupied by powerful foreign kingdoms such as Ammon and Moab. To the west of the Jordan lies the land of Canaan proper.

From the below-sea-level elevation of the river valley, the land often rises dramatically into desert-like highlands

## Giants in the Bible

According to the Book of Genesis in the Old Testament, giants lived on Earth before the Great Flood. The Rephaites ("giants") may have been a race of tall, big-boned people. Josephus Flavius, the noted Jewish historian who wrote books for Roman audiences during the first century, wrote that they had "bodies so large, and countenance so entirely different from other men, that they were surprising to the sight, and terrible to the hearing." He further wrote that they were "unlike to any credible relations to other men." Of course, Josephus was recounting Jewish legends, but he said the bones of the giants were still on display in his day.

The Rephaites lived between the Nile and Euphrates Rivers during Abraham's time, and this is the land that God gave to Abraham, according to Genesis 15:18–20.

The most well-known giant of all times is Goliath, the Philistine warrior who Israel's young, future king, David, felled with a stone from his slingshot. When someone uses the expression "David versus Goliath" it is understood to mean that a battle or contest is lopsided, with one side seemingly far superior to another.

*The Israelites had to cross the Jordan River to enter Canaan.*

and what is termed the central mountain spine, which can reach elevations of more than 3000 feet. From there the land begins to slope downward and westward into an area of foothills and valleys known as the Shephelah. It is these latter two regions which form the heartland of ancient Israel, and it is in the Shephelah where Samson is born and grows to manhood. Finally, again moving westward, we descend from foothills to the fertile coastal plain that ends on the shores of the Mediterranean Sea. At its southern end lies Philistia, the land of the Philistines.

## THE PROMISED LAND DIVIDED

Joshua divided up Canaan among the twelve tribes of Israel (Joshua 13–21). "These tribes were like big extended families with the oldest male (father) serving as the center of authority. As the tribes took ownership of the

*The Dead Sea is the lowest point on earth, and its waters are the world's saltiest. The average saline content of ocean water is about 3.5 percent; the waters of the Dead Sea are 26 to 35 percent salt. In fact, the salt concentration is so high that while it is possible to float in the water, it is nearly impossible to swim in it.*

pieces of the land, they settled down to build towns, grow crops, and raise herds of sheep and goats. The land these tribes owned was believed to have been assigned by God, and so no one was to sell or give their property to anyone else. If that did happen, the land was to eventually be given back to the tribe God first gave it to. This would happen during the Year of the Celebration which was celebrated approximately every fifty years."

The land east of the Jordan River went to the tribes of Reuben, Gad, and one half of the tribe of Manasseh. The land west of the Jordan went to Judah, Ephraim, the other half of the tribe of Manasseh, Benjamin, Simeon, Zebulun, Issachar, Asher, Naphtali, and Dan.

The only tribe that did not receive land was the tribe of Levi. Instead, the men of this tribe became the priests of Israel, meaning they were in charge of offering sacrifices to God. The other tribes were expected to provide the sacrifices, and the Levites could keep some of the sacrifices for themselves.

## A Geographical and Cultural Land Bridge

Because of Canaan's strategic location as a land bridge between the continents of Asia and Africa, the Israelites were highly susceptible to influences from foreign cultures. Moreover, these neighboring societies were often superior to the Israelites, agriculturally, commercially, and technologically; so their advanced ways would no doubt have been attractive to the Israelites.

But God did not want the Israelites to assimilate into these groups, or even tolerate their pagan ways. Instead, God intended for the Israelites to conquer Canaan.

Under Joshua's military leadership, the Israelites managed to conquer large portions of their Promised Land. They succeeded in taking the Transjordan—those lands on the eastern bank of the Jordan River—and the central highlands and foothills on the river's west side, and they had gained control of the hilly regions to the west and north of the Sea of Galilee. More specifically, Joshua had succeeded in taking possession of Hazor, Merom, Jericho, Ai, Achan, Gerizim and Ebal, Gibeon, Ajalon, and Makkedah:

> "The Lord gave them rest on every side just as he had sworn to their forefathers. Not one of all their enemies withstood them; the Lord handed all their enemies over to them. Not one of all the good

promises to the house of Israel failed; everyone was fulfilled." (Joshua 21:44–45)

But the Israelites did not take full possession of Canaan, and that was a mistake. There was still much to be done: the fertile lands of the plain that stretches north and south along the Mediterranean coast, and the broad and rich Jezreel valley, located between the mountain ranges of the north, remained in the hands of Israel's enemies. While the military tactics of the Israelite army may have worked well in the more difficult terrain of the highland areas, on the plains the technological advantages offered by the iron chariots of enemies like the Philistines effectively shut down the once-rapid advance of the new conquerors.

In time, rather than continue their military campaigns to overpower other tribes, the Israelites began to freely mix with their neighbors; among other things, they added some of their ritualistic cult practices to their sacred worship services, and intermarried.

"The religious system [in Canaan] was a highly organized and central element in every aspect of the daily life of the Canaanites, and its influence extended widely into the economic, political, and social spheres. The priests constituted an important and powerful group in the upper class of Canaanite society. There were landowners, slaveowners, and money-lenders on a large scale, operating within the temples and under the protection of the gods.

"In Canaan, as in Mesopotamia and Egypt, the temples were heavily endowed with landed properties and received a tremendous income. At certain periods they probably owned nearly all the land of the country and acquired almost an economic strangle-hold over the people."

This was in sharp contrast to Israelite practices concerning land. "The Israelites rejected the Canaanite aristocracy as well as the Canaanite monarchy. The land belonged to Yahweh, and Israel was a tenant. It was apportioned among the tribes and within the tribes to individual owners."

God sent Moses, Joshua, and prophets to remind the Israelites to stay strong in their faith, serve God, and adhere to the laws of God, as given to Moses. To do otherwise would jeopardize their covenant with God.

Joshua tried to keep the Israelites focused on the source of their strength and power, but this task proved as

*Bronze bulls of Canaanite origin, found in the Jordan Valley. These date from the time that the Philistines ruled the coast of Canaan. The polytheistic people of Canaan worshipped bulls as symbols of strength and fertility.*

Joshua led the Israelites to a victory over the Canaanites at Jericho. God knocked down the city's strong walls, enabling the Israelites to capture the fortified city.

difficult to manage as the military campaigns he pursued. Before his death, Joshua gave the Israelites a final admonition:

> So be very careful to love the Lord your God. But if you turn away and ally yourselves with the survivors of these nations that remain among you and if you intermarry with them and associate with them, then you may be sure that the Lord your God will no longer drive out these nations before you. Instead, they will become snares and traps for you, whips on your back and thorns in your eyes, until you perish from this good land, which the Lord your God has given you. (Joshua 23:11–13)

## LOCAL MILITARY HEROES

Joshua led the Israelites for about twenty-five years. At the time of his death there was still much territory left to seize. This is where things stand when the Book of Judges opens.

Judges covers the history of Israel between the death of Joshua and the rise of the monarchy. It is a tumultuous and uncertain time, in which the Israelites battle for control of the land of Canaan; in doing so, they find themselves pitted against their neighbors and main adversaries, the Philistines.

It was during the period of the Judges, according to Bible scholars, that the use of the term "Israel" (or "Israelites") began to replace the term "Hebrew," in the same way that the term "Jews" and "Judeans" will come to replace the term "Israelites."

The Judges were primarily local military heroes, natural leaders. They exercised leadership over a population that "conveniently adapted their way of life to the

Canaanite practices, especially those which were aimed at the maintenance and improvement of their well being." The author(s) of Judges blames Israel's misfortune during this period of settlement on the population at large, because the Israelites rejected God. Many mixed their worship of God with rituals from the cults of Baal, Asherah, Ashtoreth, and other Canaanite gods.

"The age of the Judges was one during which the ties, binding the Israelites together in the wilderness, had relaxed," F. J. Foakes-Jackson writes in *Biblical History of the Hebrews*. "As long as the people were under the stern discipline of the desert, ruled by a Moses, or a Joshua, constantly within sight of the national sanctuary, they made steady progress.

"But once they were in possession of a territory of their own, and each tribe lived in isolation, discipline became relaxed, and the pure worship of Jehovah began to be corrupted by the idolatrous practices of the Canaanites. The consequence was that the strength of Israel rapidly waned; the nation seemed not only unable to conquer new territories, but incapable of holding its own; there was little united action among the tribes, and less and less of the spirit of true religion. With the decay of Israel's faith the whole fabric of society was threatened with dissolution, and the legends of the period, preserved by the compiler of the Judges, show to what a state the Chosen Race had sunk."

# THE PHILISTINES

The Bible is the source of the most complete written records about the Philistines. Still, pinpointing their origins is complicated. Archaeologists and historians offer competing theories to explain where they came from, and when and how they arrived. Most theories arrive at one likely conclusion: "The biblical Philistines can best be defined as the descendants and inheritors of the highly sophisticated and cosmopolitan culture of the Late Bronze Age Aegean world."

Nearly all theories place the original homeland of the Philistines somewhere in the eastern end of the Mediterranean Sea. Some scholars argue for a location that lies more westerly in the Aegean Sea area, including the mainland of Greece and the island of Crete, site of the fabled Minoan civilization. Others propose that archaeological and linguistic evidence points to Asia Minor—known also as Anatolia, and now modern-day

*The ruins of Carthage, an ancient city settled by the Sea People on the coast of North Africa, in present-day Tunisia. Carthage was established hundreds of years after the events described in the biblical Book of Judges—possibly by descendants of the Philistines who left Canaan after the ultimate Israelite conquest.*

Turkey—either on the mainland or one of the many islands off its western coast. Still others locate the Philistines' origin even farther east, along the southeastern coast of Asia Minor or on the island of Cyprus, barely one hundred nautical miles from the coast of Canaan.

Why the Philistines migrated from their homeland is a mystery lost to time. To leave one's home and venture to new and unknown lands has always been a serious undertaking, and the fact that this appears to have been a mass migration strongly suggests that external rather than internal influences led to such a large scale movement of people and goods. And indeed, the period immediately preceding that of Philistine settlement in Canaan (different theories place them here from about 1200 B.C.E. to somewhere around the middle of the next century) was one of great change and instability.

"The history of this area during the Late Bronze Age was full of momentous events," writes Neal Bierling in his study *Philistines: Giving Goliath His Due*. "The last half of the thirteenth century B.C.E. witnessed the collapse of the Hittite empire in Anatolia, the Trojan War, the collapse of Aegean civilization and culture at numerous Greek mainland and island sites, and the end of Egypt's domination over Syro-Palestine."

What exactly happened to produce this overwhelming disruption has been the subject of intense scholarly debate, and again many theories have been proposed: internal political turmoil or outside attacks by migrating invaders; geological activity which produced massive earthquakes throughout the region, and possibly even a volcanic eruption and resulting tidal wave that destroyed the Minoan civilization on Crete; more gradual but just as serious problems with drought caused by climate change; and finally, technological innovations such as iron weapons.

## THE SEA PEOPLES

Whatever their reasons for moving around, the Philistines were very much a force to be reckoned with. These migrating "Sea Peoples," as the Egyptians called them, had an aggressive military policy and superior arms.

They had launched a series of invasions of Egypt and surrounding coastal areas somewhere around the last third of the thirteenth century B.C.E., but they failed to penetrate Egypt. Their definitive defeat by Egypt's pharaoh Ramses III around 1190 B.C.E. is recorded in both written records and in vivid picture reliefs found on the walls of the temple at Medinet Habu in Egypt. According to the official account by the Pharaoh, the Philistines and their allies were "made ashes," utterly destroyed, and it was Ramses who generously raised them up from their ruin by resettling them, perhaps as vassals, on the southern coastal plain of Canaan. However, archaeologist Neal Bierling suggests that this "boast may have been an after-the-fact government 'spin' that some of the Sea Peoples had settled in Canaan," and that it was Ramses' way of saving face in a situation over which he may have had little control.

Evidence unearthed by archaeologists shows clearly that radical change was occurring in the cities of the coastal plain beginning in the twelfth century B.C.E. Many cities show a layer of destruction below a later rebuilding and expansion. Whether there was a wave of invasion and destruction by the Philistines and their allies or whether these cities were already in decline because of other political circumstances is not clear, but what is clear is that when the Philistines arrived, they came with the knowledge and the ability to rebuild and reshape the cities they found into powerful and prosperous urban centers.

"They were accomplished architects and builders, highly artistic pottery makers, textile manufacturers, dyers, metalworkers, silver smelters, and farmers, soldiers and sophisticated urban planners," according to archaeologists Trude and Moshe Dothan, authors of *People of the Sea: The Search for the Philistines*. "They played no small part in influencing the culture and political organization of their neighbors."

*This gold and carnelian necklace of Philistine origin was excavated from a cemetery near Gaza. It dates from the late Bronze Age or early Iron Age.*

## Five Powerful City-States

The Philistines' origins may remain uncertain, as well as their reasons for migrating, but what's known is they succeeded in gaining a hold on the coastal plain of Canaan. They impeded Israel's development as a nation, and made life unbearable for the Israelites for almost two hundred years.

"Their closely knit political structure, coupled with the need for mercantile expansion, brought the Philistines into the hinterland." This put the Israelites "squarely in the path of the Philistines' drive to the east. Various Israelite tribes were badly hit by the systematic depradation of the strangers from the coast. Eventually the situation reached such a pass that the tribes most seriously affected were driven to submit to a central authority."

This is the world into which Samson was born. His people, the Israelites, were no match for the Philistines, whose society was divided up into five important city-states (Gaza, Ashkelon, Ashdod, Ekron, and Gath), which would unite for military attacks. Led by warlords, or seranim, the Philistine military included foot soldiers, horsemen, archers, and charioteers. "Moreover, the Philistines had a virtual monopoly on the important new metal, iron, and used it for swords, ax heads, and chariots, as well as for plough tips and sickles."

The Israelite tribes, by comparison, were not united as a nation. Instead, each tribe operated independently, with each tribe in control of a specific area. Or, as the last verse of Judges records, "In those days there was no king in Israel: every man did that which was right in his own eyes" (Judges 21:25).

# THE JUDGES

The Book of Judges spans about 325 years, from the death of Joshua around 1375 B.C.E. to 1050 B.C.E., the beginning of the monarchy. Samson ruled only twenty of those years, yet Bible readers are told more about Samson than any other figure in the book, and the Spirit of God is mentioned in connection with his name more than the other judges. Even so, Samson is altogether different from the other judges.

After the death of their leader Joshua, the Israelites had mixed success in driving out other groups from Canaan. This was not good; the Lord had commanded them to rid the land of all others. Because they disobeyed this command, God sent an angel with a message for the Israelites:

> I promised your ancestors that I would give this land to their families, and I brought your people here from Egypt. We made an agreement that I promised

## 42 *Samson*

This illustrated page from a 13th-century French Bible depicts scenes from the Book of Judges. (Top) The children of Israel forsake God for the foreign deities Baal and Ashtoreth. (Second) God chooses Ehud as Israelite leader. (Third) Eglon is slain. (Fourth) Israelites go to Deborah for judgement, and she fights Sisera with Barak.

> never to break, and you promised not to make any peace treaties with the other nations that live in the land. Besides that, you agreed to tear down the altars where they sacrifice to their idols. But you didn't keep your promise.
>
> And so, I'll stop helping you defeat your enemies. Instead, they will be there to trap you into worshipping their idols (Judges 2:1–3).

Despite His anger toward the Israelites, God raised up judges to deliver them from their oppressors. The first judge was Othniel, a nephew and son-in-law of Caleb, one of the twelve spies that Moses had sent to survey Canaan before the Israelites' invasion. Othniel defeated the king of Mesopotamia.

Ehud of the tribe of Benjamin was chosen by God to deliver Israel from Moab—a powerful and independent country to the northeast of the Dead Sea. This second judge was left-handed, and in Old Testament times God often bestowed special blessings on left-handed warriors. According to the account in the third chapter of the Book of Judges, Ehud stabbed the fat king of the Moabites, Eglon, with a double-edged dagger. Then he fled to the hill country of Ephraim. There, he raised an army, attacked the Moabites, killed 10,000 of the enemy, and as a result, brought peace to the land for eighty years.

After the victories of Ehud and of Shamgar, the third judge, who used an ox goad to slaughter six hundred Philistines, Israel once again fell victim to oppression by the northern Canaanities. This went on for twenty years. The ruler of the northern Canaanites was King Jabin. He ruled from the city of Hazor, to the north of the Sea of Galilee, and he had a general named Sisera, who commanded nine hundred iron chariots as well as a powerful army.

During this period of distress Israel is judged by a woman named Deborah. She summons Barak, both a judge and a soldier of the tribe of Naphtali, to inform him of God's instructions: Barak is to gather 10,000 men from his own tribe and that of Zebulun and lead them to Mount Tabor, in the Jezreel valley, to battle Sisera.

Barak says to Deborah, "'If you will go with me, I will go; but if you don't go with me, I won't go'" (Judges 4:8). Deborah agrees to go with him, but she warns him that victory over Sisera will not belong to him, but to a woman.

The rout is complete and almost total—the chariots become bogged down and mired in the mud of the River Kishon. The enemy army is destroyed; the only man who survives is Sisera, who gets down out of his chariot and flees for his life. He heads north along the valley of the Jordan, and comes upon the tent of Heber the Kenite, a man who is at peace with Sisera's king. Heber is not there, but his wife Jael is, and she is alone. She lulls Sisera to sleep and then drives a tent peg into his brain. Jael emerges from her tent to meet the approaching Barak, and triumphantly leads him back in to show him the dead enemy leader. Deborah and Barak rejoice, singing a duet of deliverance, and peace returns again for forty years.

It appears that Sisera's chariots became stuck in the mud that resulted from either a torrential rainstorm or a flash flood that came down the river. Natural phenomena have often played a decisive role in the outcome of battles. In ancient times, such events were often interpreted by the victorious side as a sign of divine favor or assistance.

*This mosaic from a Russian cathedral depicts Michael the Archangel accompanying Gideon into battle against the Midianites.*

## THE MIDIANITES

After Barak's death, Gideon becomes the fifth judge of Israel. Israel has once again returned to idol worship, so God has delivered the Israelites into the hands of the Midianites for seven years. Midianite raiders destroy crops and fields and make off with the Israelites' herd animals. The Angel of the Lord finds Gideon threshing wheat by hand in the bottom of a grape press, out of sight of any raiders. "The Lord is with you, mighty warrior," the angel says in Judges 6:12. Gideon responds:

> "Pray, sir, if the Lord is with us, why then has all this befallen us? And where are all his wonderful

deeds which our fathers recounted to us, saying, 'Did not the Lord bring us up from Egypt?' But now the Lord has cast us off, and given us into the hand of Midian." (Judges 6:13)

God commissions Gideon to defeat the Midianites. Gideon assembles an army of 32,000 men, but God tells him that is too many, for if they win they will attribute their victory to their own might, not God's. Eventually, Gideon cuts down the size to three hundred, and the three hundred face 135,000—"the Midianites and the Amalekites and all the people of the East lay along the valley like locusts for multitude; and their camels were without number, as the sand which is upon the seashore for multitude" (Judges 7:12). Nevertheless, Gideon's small army prevails, and Israel has peace for forty years.

Despite these victories, the Israelites cannot seem to stop the repeated cycles of sin and redemption. Gideon dies, and Israel returns rapidly to its worship of false gods. The sixth judge is Tola, under whose rule Israel has twenty-three years of peace; Jair follows Tola. As the seventh judge, he and his thirty sons deliver thirty Israeli cities from oppression.

After Jair's reign, a new front in the war now begins to open: Abimelech, one of Gideon's seventy-one sons, slays all but one of his seventy brothers and sets himself up as judge of Israel. After three bloody years of fighting his own countrymen, Abimelech's rule ends as he prepares to set fire to a tower full of refugees: a desperate woman drops a millstone on him, crushing his skull. The family bloodshed continues several judges later with Jephthah, who vows that if he is given a victory over the Ammonites, he will sacrifice to God whoever comes out to greet him first on his return home. It is his only daughter who comes out joyfully singing and dancing. Jephthah's judgeship is further marred by a feud that breaks out between his tribe and that of Ephraim; by the time it is over, 42,000 men of Ephraim are dead at the hand of Jephthah's tribe.

After Jephthah, a judge named Ibzan rules during seven years of peace, followed by Elon and then Abdon. Israel's next deliverer, the one who will begin to free Israel from its newest oppressor—the Philistines—is Samson.

# The Birth of Samson

According to the Bible, God set in motion a special plan for Samson's life, even before he was born. That plan centered on God using Samson to stir up trouble with the Philistines, with the long-term goal of delivering the Israelites from their Philistine oppressors.

The Angel of the Lord prophesied Samson's birth, and of all the characters in the Bible, he is one of only four biblical greats whose life story begins in such an extraordinary, divine way. The other three are Isaac, Abraham's son by his wife Sarah; John the Baptist, and Jesus Christ. Three angels prophesied the birth of Isaac, the angel Gabriel announced the birth of John the Baptist, and the Angel of the Lord, whom many Christians believe is God incarnate, told Mary, the mother of Jesus, that she would give birth to a son.

According to the scriptures, Samson's father was a man named Manoah, of the tribe of Dan. His mother's name is not

# The Birth of Samson

## Angels in the Bible

In the Bible, angels are mentioned in thirty-four books for a total of some 273 times. Angels are invisible and innumerable spirit beings that were created by God. They are inferior to God, superior to men, and possess personalities. They protect, comfort, minister to believers at the moment of death, and they inform, instruct and interpret the Word of God.

The Hebrews of Solomon's time believed there were four great angels: Gabriel, who reveals the secrets of God to men; Michael, who fights God's foes; Raphael, who receives the departing spirits of the dead; and Uriel, who summons people to judgment.

There are several different types of angels: archangels (Gabriel is an archangel whose name means "the mighty one of God"), cherubim, seraphim, ruling angels, guardian angels, and angels associated with horses and chariots. The devil is believed to be an evil, or fallen, angel.

Belief in angels is not confined to Judeo-Christian culture. Many ancient peoples, including the Egyptians and Greeks, believed in angels. Muslims also believe in angels.

*An angel holds the flame of eternal life. Detail from a mosaic in Milan, Italy.*

given; she is referred to only as Manoah's wife. They lived in Zorah, a farming village on a low hillside, not far from Philistine territory. Nothing much is revealed about the two, other than that the wife is barren. With no more information than this the narrator tells us that "the Angel of the Lord appeared to the woman and said to her, 'Behold, you are barren and have no children; but you shall conceive and bear a son'" (Judges 13:3).

The angel further instructs the wife not to drink any

## Childless Women in the Bible

In the Bible, there are several examples of women who have a difficult time conceiving and bearing children. The three patriarchs of Genesis—Abraham, Isaac, and Jacob—each had wives who were unable to give birth to children. Abraham's wife Sarah gives her Egyptian maid Hagar to Abraham as a second wife; Rachel gives her maid Bilhah to Jacob. It is Rachel who expresses most directly the terrible desperation she feels about her childless state: "'Give me children, or I shall die!'" she cries to Jacob (Genesis 30:1). But although we do not know why each wife is barren, we do know that it is God who will adjust or overcome the rules of nature.

Isaac and Rebekah endure twenty years of childlessness before Isaac's prayer is answered; only after Rachel has watched not only her elder sister but two maids bear Jacob eleven children—ten sons and a daughter—"then God remembered Rachel, and God hearkened to her and opened her womb" (Genesis 30:22). Joseph will be Rachel's firstborn; but she will die after giving birth to her second child, Benjamin.

Certainly, the most spectacular example of God's reworking of the laws of nature is when Sarah conceives and gives birth at the age of ninety. This divine birth is the beginning of the fulfillment of God's covenant with Abraham.

wine or other strong drink, and she is not to eat any food that is considered unclean according to the dietary restrictions laid down by Moses in the book of Leviticus. The angel then says that she will give birth to a son, and he is to be a Nazirite.

While the book of Numbers indicates that such a vow is to be only for a specific period of time, Manoah's wife tells her husband that their son will be a Nazirite "from birth to the day of his death."

Lastly, the angel announces that Samson or Shimshon (Hebrew, meaning "little sun") "shall begin to deliver Israel from the hand of the Philistines" (Judges 13:5).

Like his mother, this boy must refrain from wine and strong drink; indeed, anything at all to do with grapes—juice, raisins, or even vinegar. He must also carefully avoid contact with any dead body, even if it is that of his own mother or father or sibling; neither is he allowed to shave nor cut the locks of his hair.

The woman reports what happened to her husband, saying "a man of God came to me, and his countenance was like the countenance of the angel of God, very terrible; I did not ask him whence he was, and he did not tell me his name" (Judges 13:6).

Manoah, for reasons the Bible does not reveal, prays to God for the angel's return. More specifically, he asks God to send His messenger again so the couple can learn what

> The Angel of the Lord appears eight times to different people in the Old Testament, including Abraham, Jacob, and Moses. Some Christians believe that the expression "Angel of the Lord" represents an appearance of the pre-incarnate Jesus Christ.

The Angel of the Lord appears to Samson's parents and explains how their child must be raised, as described in Judges 13. The special requirements of Nazirite life are spelled out in Numbers 6.

to do with the child. So God sends the angel a second time, but only to the wife, who once more is sitting by herself in a field. She runs to find her husband, and together they return to the place where the angel is waiting.

When he sees the stranger, Manoah asks, "Are you the man who spoke to this woman?" (Judges 13:11). He then asks the angel to repeat his instructions as to how this child should be raised, and how he should be and act. The angel tells Manoah that what should be done are the things he has already told his wife.

# The Birth of Samson 53

As custom demands, Manoah then invites the Angel of the Lord to stay for dinner, and tells him that he will prepare a succulent young goat for him. But the angel tells Manoah that if he stays, he will not eat any food; if Manoah really must do something, then he should prepare a burnt offering for God. The Bible narrative then notes that Manoah did not realize he was in the presence of an angel.

Next, Manoah asks the angel his name, so that he and his wife can honor him once their son is born. But the angel answers Manoah's question with a question: "Why do you ask my name, seeing it is wonderful?" (Judges 13:18)

Manoah then takes his freshly-prepared young goat and a cereal offering, places them upon an altar built of

*A horned altar of Hebrew origin, found near the ancient city of Megiddo. Altars like this one were used for ritual sacrifices during the Judges period in Israel. Yahweh, the God of the Old Testament, expresses his preference for animals as a sacrifice almost from the beginning: Cain, a farmer, presents the fruits of his harvest to God, while his brother Abel, a shepherd, brings unblemished lambs. Abel's offering pleases God, but "on Cain and his offering He did not look with favor" (Genesis 4:5). Also, the offering of hospitality was taken very seriously in ancient Israel. The obligation to not only treat one's guests well but to also protect them from harm is illustrated elsewhere in the Old Testament.*

stone, and sets them alight. "And when the flame went up toward heaven from the altar, the Angel of the Lord ascended in the flame of the altar while Manoah and his wife looked on; and they fell on their faces to the ground" (Judges 13:20).

The Bible does not provide any details about Samson's childhood. It simply states that he grew up, the Lord blessed him, and at times the Spirit of the Lord moved him.

# SAMSON'S REVENGE

At the beginning of Chapter Fourteen of the Book of Judges, Samson is on his way to the town of Timnah, a Philistine-controlled settlement located across the valley from Zorah, about four miles southwest of the tribe of Dan's camp. There, he sees a Philistine woman, and decides that he wants to marry her.

Back home, Samson tells his parents about the woman. But they are not pleased. "Isn't there an acceptable woman among your relatives or among all our people? Must you go to the uncircumcised Philistines to get a wife?" (Judges 14:3) The Bible narrative further records that Samson's parents did not know that this was the doing of the Lord, who has a secret purpose—an occasion to confront the Philistines.

Among other reasons, the Israelites abhorred the Philistines because they were uncircumcised. The rite of circumcision may have been first practiced by the ancient Egyptians. But it was adopted by the Canaanites and by the Israelites, too; some scholars speculate that it may have originated as a fertility rite, but the Israelites later traced it back to Abraham and considered it as a symbol of their covenant with God.

However the rite came into being, the Israelites considered the practice extremely important. The Philistines had adopted the Hebrew language and many forms of Semitic worship, but they never accepted circumcision. To the Israelites this was totally unacceptable; they saw it as further proof that their Philistine oppressors were impure.

In his book *Biblical History of the Hebrews*, F. J. Foakes-Jackson writes, "With the other nationalities the Hebrews had many points in common, and were in danger of adopting their customs, but they had no such leanings toward the Philistines. Circumcision, universally practised by the Hebrew nations and their neighbors, was neglected by the newcomers, who were accordingly branded with the epithet "uncircumcised."

## Marriage in Ancient Israel

In Samson's day, it was the custom to take a wife from one's own kin—Abraham sent his servant to find a wife for Isaac among his own family in Mesopotamia, and Isaac in turn sent his son Jacob there to find a wife.

Mixed marriages were not unheard of, however. "Marriages did take place between persons of different families, and even with foreign women," according to Roland de Vaux, author of *Ancient Israel: Its Life and Institutions*. "Esau was married to a Hittite woman (Gen. 26:34), Joseph an Egyptian (Gen. 41:45), and Moses a Midianite (Ex. 2:21). . . . These mixed marriages, made by kings for political reasons, became common among subjects also, after the settlement in Canaan. They not only tainted the purity of Israel's blood but also endangered its religious faith, and were therefore forbidden by law." However, de Vaux writes that "scant respect was paid to these prohibitions . . . and the community which returned from the Exile, continued to contract mixed marriages."

It was also the custom in Samson's day for parents to arrange marriages for their children, and for practical reasons. In those days, girls married as young as age twelve and boys, thirteen. In most cases the motivation for marriage had more to do with economics than with romance. Fathers typically received a "bride-price" for daughters. This price was paid by the prospective husband, as a form of compensation for the loss of the daughter.

Though Samson's parents protested their son's choice of a woman—someone who was not his kin, and worse yet, a daughter of the Philistines, the oppressors of the Israelites—they relented and went with him on the short four-mile trip to Timnah, to meet his intended bride and to no doubt pay the requisite dowry.

While the Bible narrative leads readers to believe that the Philistines and Israelites were enemies, with little or no civil interaction, the atmosphere of the stories of Samson gives the impression that the Israelites and Philistines moved freely back and forth between their respective settlements, and enjoyed free communications and intermarriage.

Steve Weitzman, writing in the journal *Biblical Interpretation*, makes the case that the "frontier" between the Israelites and the Philistines may have been as porous as "America's border with Mexico, a boundary transgressed every month by tens of thousands of people."

He further argues that "the various peoples living there—Philistines, Canaanites, and Israelites—seem to have interacted in ways that criss-cross the border that supposedly lay between them." He bases this view on archaeological and ancient textual evidence. "The presence of Philistine pottery at sites like Beth Shemesh and Tel Batash (identified with biblical Timnah) . . . suggests a certain degree of interaction and exchange between the inhabitants of these towns (presumably Israelites) and Philistines."

Samson faces trouble even before he reaches Timnah. While he is walking through the vineyards of the town, suddenly a young lion comes roaring toward him. The Bible says the Spirit of the Lord came upon Samson and he tears the lion apart with his bare hands, as it were a young goat. He doesn't tell his parents about this incident, and continues on to Timnah, where he talks to the woman and finds that "he liked her" (Judges 14:7).

After this meeting, Samson returns home, but marriage arrangements have been made. Perhaps Samson's visit to Timnah with his parents was to formally ask the woman to marry him. In ancient Israel, an engagement, or betrothal, could last from a few days to a full year. Nevertheless, this promise was binding, as binding as the marriage itself.

## THE RIDDLE

Next the Bible records that Samson returned to marry the Timnah woman; but on the way there he saw the lion's carcass. Inside, he found a swarm of bees and honey, and he scooped out some of the honey and ate it as he walked along. He gave some to his parents, too, but did not tell them that the honey came from inside a dead carcass of a lion.

Once in Timnah, Manoah visited his son's future bride, possibly to finalize wedding arrangements; and Samson, meanwhile, threw a big party, or wedding feast. The wed-

# Samson's Revenge    59

*Samson kills the lion while on the way to Timnah; this spectacular golden fountain is located at the palace of Tsar Peter the Great in St. Petersburg, Russia, and dates from the 1730s.*

## 60 *Samson*

*"Some time later, when [Samson] went back to marry her, he turned aside to look at the lion's carcass. In it was a swarm of bees and some honey, which he scooped out with his hands and ate as he went along. When he rejoined his parents, he gave them some, and they too ate it. But he did not tell them that he had taken the honey from the lion's carcass" (Judges 14:8–9). Samson violates his Nazirite vow by eating the honey; it is impure because it has been taken from a corpse. This painting of Samson giving pieces of honeycomb to his parents was painted in the 17th century by the Italian artist Giovanni Francesco Guercino.*

ding feast was an important part of the marriage ceremony in ancient Israel, and in this instance, the feast would last seven days. Wine was usually served at wedding feasts such as these, and Samson would have violated his Nazirite vow if he drank wine at the feast.

When the Philistines saw Samson, they brought thirty companions to be with him. Bible commentators have inferred from this number that Samson's family must have been wealthy, or of some importance, to have so many members of the bride-chamber accompanying him.

Samson surprises his companions with a riddle, and then wages a bet: "If you can give me the answer within the seven days of the feast, I will give you thirty linen garments and thirty sets of clothes. If you can't tell me the answer, you must give me thirty linen garments and thirty sets of clothes" (Judges 14:12–13).

The Philistines ask to hear the riddle, and Samson replies, "Out of the eater, something to eat; out of the strong, something sweet" (Judges 14:14).

Biblical historians say that the exchange of riddles was considered a form of ancient Near Eastern wisdom. "It was a sign of 'wisdom' to frame a riddle, and of superior wisdom to solve the riddle and cap it with another," writes John McKenzie in *The World of the Judges*.

For three days the Philistines tried to crack the riddle, but failed. So on the fourth day, the Philistines tell Samson's wife, "Coax your husband into explaining the riddle for us, or we will burn you and your father's household to death. Did you invite us here to rob us?" (Judges 14:15).

Fearful, Samson's wife begs him to reveal the answer to her, crying, "You hate me! You don't really love me. You've given my people a riddle, but you haven't told me the answer" (Judges 14:16).

Samson tells her that he hasn't even disclosed the answer to the riddle to his parents, so why would or should he reveal it to her? But Samson's wife persists, crying for seven days. Finally, on the seventh day, he breaks down and tells her the answer; she, in turn, tells

*The Dutch Master Rembrandt painted this picture (1638) of Samson posing his riddle at the wedding feast.*

her countrymen. Then, before sunset on the seventh day, the men say to Samson:

> "What is sweeter than honey?
> What is stronger than a lion?" (Judges 14:18)

Samson knew immediately that the men had gotten the answer from his bride. He accuses them, saying, "If you had not plowed with my heifer, you would not have solved my riddle" (Judges 14:18).

Next the Bible records that the Spirit of the Lord came upon Samson, giving him supernatural strength. He proceeds to go to Ashkelon; there, he strikes down thirty men, strips them of their belongings and gives their clothes to the thirty who had answered the riddle. Seething, Samson then returns to his father's home, without his bride. The bride is then given in marriage to one of the thirty men who attended the wedding feast.

Samson stormed off during his wedding feast, no doubt feeling betrayed by his new wife. However, he eventually returns to Timnah, this time during the wheat harvest season. He takes a goat with him, as a gift, and announces to his "father-in-law" that he wants to visit his wife, in her chamber, or bedroom.

The father-in-law tells Samson that he has married his daughter to one of the men at the wedding party, because he believed that Samson had left for good. "I really

*Samson threatens his Philistine father-in-law, by Rembrandt, circa 1635.* In Ancient Israel: Its Life and Institutions, *Roland de Vaux writes that "Samson's marriage has close similarities with a form found among Palestinian Arabs, in that it is a true marriage but without permanent cohabitation. The woman is mistress of her own house, and the husband, known as* joz musarrib, *'a visiting husband,' comes as a guest and brings presents."*

thought that you utterly hated her, so I gave her to your companion." The father-in-law didn't stop there. He added, "Is not her younger sister more beautiful than she? Please take her instead" (Judges 15:2).

Not surprisingly, Samson is enraged. "This time I shall be blameless in regard to the Philistines, when I do them mischief," he says (Judges 15:3). He catches three hundred foxes, ties them together in pairs by their tails, with a torch placed between the tails of each pair; he then sets the torches alight, and releases the foxes into the rich fields of grain newly harvested by the Philistine farmers. The foxes run wildly in their panic, setting fire not only to the grain and to the fields, but to the olive orchards as well. His act of vengeance destroys not only the year's harvest of foodstuffs, but the seeds for next year, and it has ruined the olive harvest for many years to come.

The Philistines quickly figure out who was behind the fire and destruction, and they get their revenge by burning to death the Timnah woman and her father. When Samson finds out what happened, he retaliates; the Bible records that "he attacked them hip and thigh with great slaughter." Then he retreats some ten miles away into the territory of the tribe of Judah, to the rock at Etam. There, he mourns his loss.

The location of both the town of Lehi and of the rock

---

Some Bible scholars believe that Samson may have used jackals to destroy the Philistines' fields, rather than foxes. Foxes live alone or in pairs, but jackals travel in packs and could be caught more easily than foxes. Jackals are still common in Palestine, especially around Joppa and Gaza.

*A grove of olive trees in present-day Israel. The olive was one of the most important agricultural products of ancient Canaan. Olives are not only a nutritious and tasty food crop, but a practical one as well: their oil had important uses as fuel for lamps and as an ingredient in cosmetics and medicines. Olive trees grow and mature slowly, and produce fruits only every other year. Samson's destruction of such valuable trees would have been a severe blow to the Philistine farmers of Timnah.*

of Etam are uncertain. The rock of Etam may lie somewhere in the northern part of the wilderness known as the Judean Desert—a very convenient location for men who wish to be left alone.

Steve Weitzman, in his article "The Samson Story as Border Fiction," argues that Samson's "riddle plays a catalytic role in [his] conflict with the Philistines. Before Samson tells it, he and the Philistines are headed toward hybridization; after all, the occasion for the riddle is Samson's marriage with a Philistine woman. In the wake of the riddle, Samson and the Philistines become bitter foes: the Philistines have to cheat to solve the riddle; and Samson retaliates by slaying thirty Philistines in Ashkelon and stealing their garments, setting off a violent cycle of revenge that culminates in mutual destruction."

# SAMSON BETRAYED

The drama doesn't end at the wedding feast. The Philistines set out for Judah and, once there, raid the town of Lehi. The men of Judah are caught completely off guard; they learn from the Philistines that it is Samson they want. Then 3,000 men of Judah search for and find Samson, in the clefts of the rock at Etam. They tell Samson that they have come to arrest him, and turn him over to the Philistines. They also remind Samson that it is the Philistines who "rule over us."

Samson asked the men of Judah not to kill him; they agree, but they bind him with rope and take him to Lehi, where the waiting Philistines begin shouting when they see Samson. At that moment, the Spirit of the Lord moves in Samson and the Bible records that the rope "became like flax that is burned with fire" and his bonds break loose from his hands. Samson then picks up the fresh jawbone of a donkey and uses it to slay a

Samson smites the Philistines with the jawbone of an ass. This wall painting was found in a Roman catacomb and dates to the early years of Christianity.

thousand Philistines. Then he says, "with the jawbone of a donkey, heaps upon heaps, with the jawbone of a donkey, I have slain a thousand men!" (Judges 15:16)

After the slaughter, Samson is thirsty and cries out to the Lord, according to the Bible narrative. The Lord hears his plea, and quenches his thirst. Afterwards, Samson's spirit is revived, and the last line of Judges' Chapter Fifteen records that he judged Israel twenty years during the days of the Philistines.

## THE THIRD BETRAYAL OF SAMSON

Chapter Sixteen opens with Samson in Gaza, one of the five principle cities of the Philistines. There, he meets a prostitute and spends the night with her. When the people of Gaza find out that he is there, they plot to kill him at sunrise.

But Samson arises at midnight, and in the darkness goes to the town gate. Instead of forcing the doors of the gate open, Samson removes the doors of the gate as well as the gate posts. He then places them on his shoulders, and carries them about forty miles to the top of a hill that overlooks Hebron. He sets the doors down, still closed and locked.

The Bible narrative next switches to sometime later. It records that Samson falls in love with a woman in the Sorek Valley, a rich and fertile area near Samson's birthplace. The woman's name is Delilah.

The Book of Judges does not say whether Delilah is an Israelite or a Philistine. While many scholars have tried to argue that she is one or the other, there is no definitive answer offered by Judges.

What is known, according to the Bible, is that Philistine leaders approach Delilah with a proposition to snare Samson: "Entice him, and see wherein his great strength lies, and by what means we may overpower him, that we may bind him to subdue him; and we will each give you eleven hundred pieces of silver" (Judges 16:5).

Eleven hundred pieces of silver is an exorbitant amount, so much so that some scholars have questioned whether an error occurred when translating the saga of Samson from Hebrew to English. Abraham paid four hundred shekels for a family burial place; King David, who lived long after the time of Samson, paid fifty shekels for the oxen and threshing floor of Araunah, and the prophet Jeremiah paid seventeen shekels for a piece of property. Even if Delilah's bribe were only half of the stated amount, it still shows how important Samson's capture was to the Philistines.

70 *Samson*

*This illustration from an Italian manuscript, circa 1430, shows Samson carrying away the city gates of Gaza.*

Delilah doesn't hesitate to accept the bribe. She asks Samson, "Please tell me wherein your great strength lies, and how you might be bound, that one could subdue you" (Judges 16:6).

Samson knows better. He tells her that if he is bound with seven fresh bowstrings, he will lose his strength. Delilah relays the message to the Philistines. Then she hides the men who will seize Samson in an inner room. She binds her lover—presumably as he sleeps—and then says to him, "'The Philistines are upon you, Samson!'" (Judges 16:9).

Samson easily snaps the bowstrings. He has lied to her, and she knows it, and she protests loudly. Samson continues to play along: he tells her to use new ropes, then to weave the locks of his hair onto a loom. Each time Delilah follows his instructions, only to discover the same results: he has mocked her yet again.

## THE SECRET REVEALED

But Delilah has not given up: she "pressed him hard with her words day after day, and urged him." (Judges 16: 16). And at last her strategy works. Finally, Samson reveals to her that "a razor has never come upon my head; for I have been a Nazirite to God from my mother's womb. If I be shaved, then my strength will leave me, and I shall become weak, and be like any other man" (Judges 16:17).

This time Delilah knows that Samson has at last told her the truth. She tells the Philistines to bring their money, and has a man with a razor standing by. The next time Samson falls asleep on her lap, she has the man come in and shave off his seven locks of hair. Delilah calls out yet again, "The Philistines are upon you, Samson!"

Samson awakens and finds that his strength has gone from him; the Lord does not come to his rescue. The

Philistines seize him, gouge out his eyes, and haul him off to a prison in Gaza, where they put him to work turning a millstone to grind grain. Delilah disappears, her mission accomplished.

## THE PHILISTINES CELEBRATE

The Philistines sometime later throw a party, to honor their god Dagon, who they believe has delivered "our enemy into our hand, the ravager of our country, who has slain many of us" (Judges 16:24). According to biblical historians, the Philistines worshipped many gods, including Dagon, Ashtoreth, and Baal-zebub. Ashtoreth was a goddess of love and fertility, while Baal-zebub was the principal god of the Philistine city of Ekron—in Judeo-Christian tradition, this deity has sometimes been associated with Lucifer and the fallen angels of Hell. The Philistines considered Dagon to be one of the most important and highest-ranking gods, however.

The Philistines employed soothsayers and diviners to interpret the wishes of their many gods, and they often carried small idols representing certain gods into battle. They built temples where the gods could be worshipped. Large temples to Dagon existed in many Philistine cities, including Ashdod, Beth-dagon, and Gaza.

## REJOICING, UNTO DEATH

As the Philistines' celebration in the temple proceeds, they called for someone to bring Samson. When the humiliated judge arrives, he is mocked and laughed at, while the Philistines celebrate their victory over him.

Samson stands, surrounded by the laughing, rejoicing Philistine crowd—thousands in the temple itself, and some 3,000 on the roof. He realizes that he is in the center of the temple, between the two massive pillars that

# Samson Betrayed

*The Venetian Renaissance artist Andrea Mantegna created this painting of Samson and Delilah around 1495.*

## 74 Samson

Samson destroys the temple of Dagon, as described in Judges 16:25–30: "When they stood him among the pillars, Samson said to the servant who held his hand, 'Put me where I can feel the pillars that support the temple, so that I may lean against them.' . . . Then Samson reached toward the two central pillars on which the temple stood. Bracing himself against them, his right hand on the one and his left hand on the other, Samson said, 'Let me die with the Philistines!' Then he pushed with all his might, and down came the temple on the rulers and all the people in it. Thus he killed many more when he died than while he lived."

support the entire structure. He prays: "Please remember me, Lord God. The Philistines poked out my eyes, but make me strong one last time, so I can take revenge for at least one of my eyes!" (Judges 16:28).

God listens, and then Samson grasps the two columns holding up the roof. Next he shouts, "Let me die with the Philistines!" (Judges 16:30).

The temple collapsed, and the Bible records that Samson killed more Philistines when he died than he had killed during his entire life. Samson's brothers and father, and perhaps the whole tribe of Dan, brought him back from Gaza and buried him in a place between Zorah and Eshtaol.

## WOMEN IN THE BIBLE

It might be said that Samson was unlucky when it came to women. His Timnah wife let him down, and his lover Delilah betrayed him for silver. The only other women that the Bible associates with Samson are his mother and a nameless prostitute.

Samson's mother is never named in the Book of Judges. But the Jewish historian Flavius Josephus wrote that Samson's mother was "remarkably beautiful." Josephus also suggested in his writings from antiquity that her husband was a jealous man. "The woman told Manoah about the angel's visit and message. But he became jealous and would not believe it, so his wife asked God to send the angel again, that her husband might also see him. When the angel appeared to her again, she called Manoah, and although he saw the angel, he was still suspicious."

Though little is known of Samson's mother, biblical scholars in recent history have at least credited her with being a woman who was more sensible and perceptive than her husband.

"Manoah's faith is traditional and rational, but slow to recognize the presence of God. . . . The woman (Judges 13:3), on the other hand, has an intuitive faith. Sensing the supernatural character of the stranger, she accepts his words without asking details about his name or origin (v. 6), knowing in her heart that 'God cannot be expressed but only addressed.'"

Throughout Samson's entire story, as well as in many of the episodes of Judges, women are very active participants in major and often formative events in the establishment of Israel. The judge Deborah is an example, though at first she takes on a more secondary role to that of Barak.

Many artists have produced paintings or sculptures that depict scenes from the story of Samson and Delilah. This painting by the 17th-century Dutch master Anthony van Dyck shows the Philistines arresting Samson after his hair has been cut by Delilah.

The one woman who stands out from all the rest, of course, is Delilah—"immortalized as the temptress par excellence, the femme fatale, the seductive siren, the whore." Almost nothing is known about Delilah. Though it is assumed by some Bible commentators that she is a seductress, or even a prostitute, this is not stated in the Bible. What is known, however, is that Delilah has her own residence, because the Bible says Samson visited her there; and while some have speculated that it was a house of prostitution, again no such information is provided in the biblical narrative.

Modern scholars, particularly women scholars, have offered new perspectives on Delilah's actions. For example, Danna Nolan Fewell, a professor of Hebrew Bible at Drew Theological School and the Casperson School of Graduate Studies in New Jersey, has suggested that Delilah was simply a woman looking after her own financial needs:

> Delilah's identity is not bound to any man. Introduced simply by name, she is a woman who takes care of herself. She conducts her love affair with Samson and her business affairs with the lords of the Philistines without any father, brother, or husband acting as a mediator. The narrator says that Samson loves Delilah. How Delilah feels about him is not revealed. . . . Eleven hundred pieces of silver from each Philistine nobleman are promised for information on how Samson might be subdued. Doubtless, as a woman alone, Delilah finds that the love of a wanted man is no match for the security of wealth.

Fewell casts a different light on Samson's wife as well as the harlot he visited. In her view, both of the women were simply taking care of their own self-interests, and Fewell argues that self-interest is a strong motivator:

> A prostitute is a businesswoman, a woman who uses her sexuality as a means of feeding or clothing herself. She does what she does in order to ensure her survival. The bride and Delilah behave in like manner. They do what they do in order to survive.
>
> The bride attempts (unsuccessfully) to protect herself and her family from the threat of death. Delilah, a woman without a father, brother, or husband to support her, secures her financial stability.

The short book that follows Judges, the book of Ruth, is exclusively about two women—about their relationship, how they comfort and sustain each other during extreme hardship, and how they even manage to continue the family line when their own husbands have failed to do so. This unusual cluster of stories that focus on women has led one critic to propose that Judges may have been written by a woman:

> The humans who serve, some well, some minimally, are primarily men who have a tendency to get carried away with their self-importance—that is to behave as if they are gods. The standard of faith is embodied by three extraordinary women—Deborah, Jael and Jephthah's daughter. This standard combined with the low status of women [ . . . ] supports the possibility of a woman storyteller satirizing humans who play God.

In Samson's case, the truth and details about the women in his life lay buried with him in the tomb of Manoah his father.

# SAMSON: THE MYTH AND THE MAN

In many ways, the saga of Samson is the saga of Israel. God loved Samson, in spite of his flaws and weaknesses, and God loved the Israelites, in spite of their flaws and weaknesses.

"In Jewish History and legend his name evokes the fantastic," writes Elie Wiesel in *Wise Men and their Tales: Portraits of Biblical, Talmudic, and Hasidic Masters*. "He is Samson, or Shimshon, the heroic warrior who prevails over nature and its laws, over men and their aspirations to grandeur and conquest. He laughed at his enemies, whom he effortlessly vanquished. Nothing frightened him. The most savage beasts feared him. With one hand he was capable of reducing an entire mountain to dust. With both he gathered three hundred foxes and fastened torches to them to bring fire to enemy fields. His only weakness? Women. He could stand up to mighty adversaries, but yielded quickly to their charm and their beauty.

"And yet he was a Nazir, a Nazirite, an ascetic man consecrated to God, one of God's chosen. A man whom God needed to avenge His honor and save His people. How can this be? How can a human being be made of such contradictory tendencies? On the one hand, the text describes his astonishing record as a judge in Israel; on the other hand, we frequently find him with attractive females who, moreover, are not even Jewish."

Bible interpreters and historians have attached many labels to Samson—hero, superman, wild man, deliverer, a tragic messiah, and even juvenile delinquent. And his name is forever tied to Delilah, who may have become a rich woman after accepting a bribe from the rulers of the Philistines, the enemies of the Israelites.

## THE POWERFUL PHILISTINES

"Of all the enemies of Israel in the Book of Judges, the Philistines were the most persistent and, in the long run, most threatening," according to E. John Hamlin, author of *At Risk in the Promised Land: A Commentary on the Book of Judges*:

> Three factors made the Philistines such a moral threat to Israelite independence: (1) their efficient political organization which made it possible for their five cities (Josh. 13:3) to act as one; (2) their military discipline; and (3) their superiority in military technology, including chariots (Judges 1:19; 1 Sam. 13:5) and a monopoly on iron weapons which gave them an advantage over the bronze weapons of the Israelites.
>
> They took over the Canaanite cities of Gaza, Ashkelon and Ashdod, and built Gath and Ekron (which ruled over Timnah . . .) further inland for military and commercial control of the approaches to the hill country. When Egyptian power declined

## Samson: the Myth and the Man    81

*This bronze sculpture of a chariot dates from early Roman times. The Philistines' superior military technology, including chariots and iron weapons, made them a strong regional power.*

under Ramses III (1195–1164), the Philistines inherited reins of power in Canaan for themselves. The Samson saga probably dates from this period of expanding Philistine ambition.

There are more than 250 references in the Bible to the Philistines—even Abraham and his son Isaac have run-ins with them. Samson, as much as anyone, tried to rid Canaan of them, though he perhaps went about it the wrong way, and for the wrong reasons. He waged what seemed to be personal vendettas against them, as opposed

*These figures at Karnak represent the Egyptian pharaoh Ramses III, considered the last great ruler of Egypt's New Kingdom. Court records during his rule report that Egyptian territory was invaded by numerous foreign armies, including the Sea People. The invaders established states like Philistia in the lands they conquered.*

## Samson: the Myth and the Man    83

to organized military campaigns, as championed by the other judges. And though he ruled for twenty years, Samson never succeeded in delivering Israel from its enemies.

"The story of the last judge begins in a way different from any of the other judges," Hamlin observes. "In the Samson saga the period of oppression is twice as long as the previous longest oppression . . . Yet there is no cry of distress, no call for deliverance, no decision to remove foreign gods and return to Yahweh. It appears that the people of Judah had accepted as unchangeable fate the fact that 'the Philistines are rulers over us' (15:11)."

It remains unclear where the Philistines came from, or even when they entered Canaan. "The evidence for Philistine origins is complex," argues David M. Howard Jr. in an article that appeared in *Peoples of the Old Testament World*. "Ultimately, it points to different peoples from different times, all of whom came to be called 'Philistines.'"

Archaeological evidence has provided some information about the Philistines: "[They] were capable farmers and artisans as can be seen from the discovery of underground silos, flint sickle blades, millstones, oil presses, loomweights, and wine jars.

"They were largely urban dwellers. Their cities were well planned and well fortified and they traded their industrial products with the rest of the Mediterranean world."

By comparison, the Israelites, after a forty-year journey through the desert and four hundred years in Egypt—a portion of the time as slaves—were no match for the Philistines. "Except for occasional brief emergency alliances, the Israelite tribes maintained complete autonomy during the Period of the Judges and recognized no central capital or shrine for all of Israel. . . . The hilly terrain, netted by a maze of valleys and wadis, made for political disjunction.

"The heads of wealthy and important families constituted a group of 'elders,' and they met—usually in the town gate, the common meeting place in those days—whenever the occasion demanded. The elders . . . made their authority felt in every aspect of the community's activities, the military, political, religious, economic, legal, and social."

But this "primitive democracy" was no match for the Philistines.

"As conquerors the Philistines acted in a totally different manner from the early oppressors," author F. J. Foakes-Jackson writes in his book, *Biblical History of the Jews*. "The Midianites and Moabites had come to plunder,

*Weapons made from iron, such as the spear point on the right, hold a sharp edge longer than weapons made from bronze (left). This gives an advantage to the army that fights with iron weapons, as they are more deadly in battle. When the Israelites entered Canaan, they did not possess the technology for smelting iron and working it into weapons.*

but the Philistines conquered to rule. They disarmed the Israelites and forced them to do their bidding. The struggle between the two nations lasted for generations, and ended in the Israelites becoming masters of Palestine. In early days, however, the tribes bordering on the territory of the Philistines were reduced to a condition of abject submission."

As warriors, the Sea Peoples, which included the Philistines, were decidedly superior to the Israelites. "The Sea Peoples fought with infantry, ships, and chariots. Each infantryman carried two spears, a round shield, and a long, straight sword, and they fought in groups of four. The chariots were pulled by horses, and each had two six-spoked wheels. They were manned by crews of three, who were armed with two long spears, like the infantry."

This is the sort of military might that the Israelites were up against. Samson's private battles against the Philistines mirrored the battles the Israelites fought against the Philistines. In both instances, the Philistines were powerful; Samson and the Israelites, powerless. Nevertheless, the Israelites had the favor of God: "Israel's strength lay in united devotion to the Lord."

## THE WEDDING RIDDLE

Samson's wedding riddle has puzzled scholars, historians, and biblical commentators for centuries. Still today, many try to decode the narrator's intent in including the riddle in the Samson saga, especially when one considers that Samson's phrase was not so much a riddle as a statement—and only he could have known what he was talking about.

Steve Weitzman, a professor of religious studies at Indiana University, suggests that the riddle was meant to explain how the Philistines lost control of the region:

At the beginning of the story, the Philistines dominate Israel, but their power begins to unravel thanks to Samson. First, they find their control of the countryside challenged when Samson burns their vineyards and olive groves. Then he assaults the boundaries of Philistine civic space by single-handedly uprooting and relocating the gates of the city of Gaza, and just when the Philistines seem about to reassert their control, Samson destroys their temple, striking at the symbolic and social core of their world. Each act of violence reaches deeper and deeper into the Philistines' settled existence, from fields to gate to temple, progressively undoing the civic and religious order they have imposed on the countryside.

Hamlin, author of *At Risk in the Promised Land: A Commentary on the Book of Judges*, offers another interpretation of the riddle.

The riddle, on its face a bawdy or ribald wedding night joke among male companions, carries deeper meanings. Out of the "eater" (the shambles of the old destructive order) comes "something to eat": the hope of *shalom*, of milk and honey in the Promised Land of the future. Out of the "strong" (the broken political, economic, and military machine) comes something "sweet": a land of olive trees and honey, a land . . . in which you will lack nothing . . . where there will be the sweetness of God's word as the guide to peace.

## CANAAN THEN AND NOW

The coastal plain of Canaan was and continues to be a very desirable location for three very fundamental reasons: it is relatively flat and open, its soils are fertile, and

*Samson: the Myth and the Man* 87

*Land rights remain the burning issue in Israel—the land once known as Canaan—even today. The Jewish people are committed to possessing the land that they believe God promised exclusively for them. However, Palestinian Arabs contest their claim.*

The Israelites did not succeed in defeating the Philistines and uniting Canaan under their control until the time of King David.

there is sufficient rainfall for crops. While the land of Canaan is geologically a land bridge connecting the continents of Europe, Asia, and Africa, its higher elevations form a natural funnel that directs traffic along the coastal plain, and this is exactly where one of the most important ancient highways was located—the Great Trunk Road or Via Maris ("The Way of the Sea").

It is therefore no surprise to read of the five great Pentapolis cities of Gaza, Ashkelon, Ashdod, Ekron, and Gath, and the commercial and military power that they represented. And, because of what we know about the geography of Canaan, it should also be no surprise to think of the very different geographical situation that lay just a few short miles to the west, in the higher regions controlled by the Israelites: less fertile soils, less rainfall, forests that needed to be cleared, a general lack of flat land that could only be remedied by the labor-intensive work of building terraces into the hillsides, and farmers fully occupied with trying to grow enough food to sustain their own families. And in between these two contrasts in geography lies the birthplace of Samson—the foothills of the Shephelah.

## THE LAST JUDGE

By all accounts, Samson was unlike any of the other judges—most scholars and historians would readily agree. His saga reads like an adventure story: every battle he waged, he waged alone. He was strong, as far as his physical strength, but weak to temptations. He was a Nazirite from birth, yet he associated with people and practices contrary to the Nazirite way of life. He was spirit-filled, yet forever yielding to carnal desires. He began his life with great promise, yet it ended tragically.

"[It] is a lively human story of passion and love corrupted by fear, corruption and bribery (Judges 14:15; 16:5); of insult and retaliation (14:20; 15:3,7,10); of flaming fields and flaming death (15:4–6); of a hero who loves to look at women; but is blinded because of his foolish love (v. 21); of a superman who can carry city gates 40 km (24 mi) uphill (v. 3); and burst unbreakable bonds four times, but who cannot break the bonds of a scheming lover; of a proud champion who twice is humbled and prays, once for life (15:18) and again for death, in order to accomplish his life's purpose (16:28, 30); of the mysterious workings of God in ways unrecognized by his own people (13:6; 14:4)."

The Reverend George Dana Boardman, a noted Baptist minister who lived from 1828 to 1903 and whose writings on ethics are still studied by Biblical scholars today, preached about the link between character and destiny. One of his sayings on the subject is often quoted today: "Sow an act and you reap a habit; sow a habit and you reap a character. Sow a character and you reap a destiny."

On the surface, it might seem that Samson charted his own destiny with his first "bad" decision to pursue a Philistine woman. However, Bible commentators who take a broad view underscore God's role in Samson's life. After all, unlike any of the other judges, Samson's birth was foretold by the Angel of the Lord. What's more, God is the source of Samson's supernatural power, according to the Bible, and His Spirit remains with Samson, irrespective of whatever troubles Samson brings upon himself—even in the face of death, God is with him.

"Samson is the muscular, intrepid, religious, rollicking Hercules of sacred story," Boardman wrote. "Witness his leonine exploit in the vineyards of Timnah; his playful riddle at the marriage feast; his boyish stratagem with the

# Samson: the Myth and the Man 91

*After Samson's death, Israel did not have strong leaders. The remaining chapters of Judges detail how the Israelites fell into idol worship and fought among themselves, rather than against their enemies. The book closes with the line, "In those days Israel had no king; everyone did as he saw fit" (Judges 21:25).*

three hundred foxes; his grotesque slaughter of the thousand Philistines with the jawbone of an ass; his prankish striding away with the gates of Gaza; his frolicsome amours with Delilah; his grim humor in the very act of suicide.

"Yet this man, so jovial and mettlesome and wayward, is mentioned in the New Testament muster-roll of the Old

*Many statues and monuments depict events from Samson's life, such as this fountain in the Czech Republic.*

Testament Sons of Faith, enshrined in the catalogue which contains such saintly names as Abel, Enoch, Abraham, Moses, Samuel, David and the prophets. Whenever we are tempted to pronounce an altogether unfavorable judgment, it is well to remember that there is One who (1 Sam. 16:7) sees not as man sees; for man looks on the outward appearance, while Jehovah looks on the heart."

## SAMSON IN POPULAR CULTURE

The character Samson lives on today in popular culture. His story has been the subject of many films and television programs. Elite Israeli combat units have been named after Samson, and Israel's nuclear program was called the "Samson Option."

Samson is even on sale in American stores. The creator of the billion-dollar G.I. Joe toy has created a new line of action figures called Almighty Heroes, and Samson is one of the biblical figures.

In the end, Samson is perhaps whatever the reader of his story chooses to make of him. "Regarding his qualities as a political and military leader, the truth is, they are hard to identify," writes Nobel Peace Prize winner Elie Wiesel. "A leader must be able to mobilize his community and motivate his soldiers. But he did everything by himself. He was always, as in the earliest days, a solitary warrior who rose up against the enemy."

Others take a different view: they cheer Samson for literally bringing down the house on the heads of Israel's oppressors. In their eyes, he is a hero. For still others, the story of Samson is certainly about a conqueror, but in their view, the superhero in the Book of Judges, as in all books of the Bible, is Almighty God.

# Notes

**CHAPTER ONE: SAMSON THE NAZIRITE**

p. 12: "Samson's name has become . . ." Rabbi Joseph Telushkin, *Jewish Literacy: The Most Important Things to Know about the Jewish Religion, Its People and Its History* (New York: W. Morrow, 1991), p. 59.

p. 14: "The stories of Samson . . ." John L. McKenzie, *The World of the Judges* (London: Geoffrey Chapman, 1967), p. 150.

p. 16: "Although Jewish tradition . . . " Telushkin, *Jewish Literacy*, p. 59.

p. 17: "Samson is a hero . . ." McKenzie, *The World of the Judges*, p. 158.

**CHAPTER TWO: JOURNEY TO THE PROMISED LAND**

p. 24: "When the Hebrews and Israelites . . ." Harry M. Orlinksy, *Ancient Israel* (Ithaca, NY: Cornell University Press, 1954), p. 52.

p. 27: "These tribes were like . . . " Howard Clark Kee, et. al, eds. *From Joshua to the Exile: The People of Israel in the Promised Land* (New York: American Bible Society, 1995), p. 907.

p. 30: "The religious system . . ." Orlinsky, *Ancient Israel*, p. 54.

p. 31: "The Israelites rejected . . ." McKenzie, *The World of the Judges*, p. 116.

p. 34: "conveniently adapted their way . . . " Orlinsky, *Ancient Israel*, p. 56.

p. 34: "The age of the Judges . . . " F. J. Foakes-Jackson,

*Biblical History of the Hebrews to the Christian Era* (Cambridge, England: W. Heffer & Sons, Ltd., 1921), p. 125.

## CHAPTER THREE: THE PHILISTINES

p. 35: "The biblical Philistines can best . . ." Ann E. Killebrew, *Biblical Peoples and Ethnicity: An Archaeological Study of Egyptians, Canaanites, Philistines, and Early Israel, 1300–1100 B.C.E.* (Leiden and Boston: Brill, 2005), p. 234.

p. 37: "The history of this area . . ." Neal Bierling, *Philistines: Giving Goliath His Due*, Marco Polo Monographs 7 (Warren Center, Pa.: Shangri-La Publications, 2002), pp. 68–69.

p. 38: "[ . . .] boast may have been . . ." Bierling, *Philistines: Giving Goliath His Due*, p. 43.

p. 38: "They were accomplished . . ." Trude Dothan and Moshe Dothan, *Peoples of the Sea: The Search for the Philistines* (New York: MacMillan Publishing Company, 1992), p. 259.

p. 39: "Their closely knit . . . " Orlinsky, *Ancient Israel*, p. 63.

p. 39: "Squarely in the path . . ." Orlinsky, *Ancient Israel*, p. 63.

p. 40: "Moreover, the Philistines . . . " Orlinsky, *Ancient Israel*, p. 63.

## CHAPTER SIX: SAMSON'S REVENGE

p. 56: "With other nationalities . . ." Foakes-Jackson, *Biblical History of the Hebrews to the Christian Era*, p. 120.

p. 56: "marriages did take place . . ." Roland de Vaux, *Ancient Israel: Its Life and Institutions*, trans. John McHugh (New York: McGraw-Hill Co., 1965), p. 31.

p. 57: "scant respect . . ." de Vaux, *Ancient Israel: Its Life and Institutions*, p. 31.

p. 57: "America's border . . ." Steve Weitzman, "The Samson Story as Border Fiction," *Biblical Interpretation* 10, no. 2 (2002), p. 158.

p. 57: "the various peoples . . ." Weitzman, "The Samson Story as Border Fiction," p. 160.

p. 58:     "The presence of Philistine . . . " Weitzman, "The Samson Story as Border Fiction," p. 160.

p. 61:     "It was a sign . . ." McKenzie, *The World of the Judges*, p. 153.

p. 63:     "Samson's marriage . . ." de Vaux, *Ancient Israel: Its Life and Institutions*, p. 29.

p. 66:     "riddle plays a catalytic . . ." Weitzman, "The Samson Story as Border Fiction," p. 165.

## CHAPTER SEVEN: SAMSON BETRAYED

p. 75:     "remarkably beautiful," Flavius Josephus, *The Essential Josephus*, trans. Paul L. Maier (Grand Rapids, Mich.: Kregel Publications, 1994), p. 93.

p. 75:     "The woman told Manoah . . ." Josephus, *The Essential Josephus*, p. 93.

p. 75:     "Manoah's faith is . . ." E. John Hamlin, *At Risk in the Promised Land: A Commentary on the Book of Judges* (Grand Rapids, Mich.: W. B. Eerdman, 1990), p. 131.

p. 76:     "immortalized as the temptress . . ." Susan Ackerman, "What If Judges Had Been Written by a Philistine?," *Biblical Interpretation* 8, no.1/2 (April 2000), p. 36.

p. 77:     "Delilah's identity . . ." D.N. Fewell, "Judges," in Carol A. Newsom and Sharon H. Ringe, eds., *Women's Bible Commentary* (Louisville, Ky.: Westminster John Knox Press, 1998), p. 79.

p. 77:     "A prostitute . . ." Fewell, "Judges," p. 80.

p. 78:     "The humans who serve . . ." Adrien Janis Bledstein, "Is Judges a Woman's Satire of Men Who Play God?" *A Feminist Companion to Judges*, ed. Athalya Brenner (Sheffield, England: Sheffield Academic Press, 1993), pp. 52–53.

## CHAPTER EIGHT: THE LEGEND OF SAMSON

p. 80:     "Of all the enemies . . ." Hamlin, *At Risk in the Promised Land: A Commentary on the Book of Judges*, p. 127.

p. 80:     "Three factors made . . . " Hamlin, *At Risk in the Promised Land: A Commentary on the Book of Judges*, p. 129.

p. 79: "In Jewish History . . ." Elie Wiesel, *Wise Men and their Tales: Portraits of Biblical, Talmudic, and Hasidic Masters* (New York: Schocken Books, 2003), p. 119.

p. 83: "The evidence for Philistine origin . . ." David M. Howard Jr., "Philistines," *Peoples of the Old Testament World* (Grand Rapids, Mich.: Baker, 1994), p. 231.

p. 83: " They were capable farmers . . ." Lawrence J. Silberstein and Robert L. Cohn, *The Other in Jewish Thought and History: Constructions of Jewish Identity and Culture* (New York: New York University Press, 1994), p. 66.

p. 83: "Except for occasional . . ." Orlinsky, *Ancient Israel*, pp. 58–61.

p. 84: "primitive democracy," Orlinsky, *Ancient Israel*, p. 61.

p. 84: "As conquerors . . ." Foakes-Jackson, *Biblical History of the Hebrews to the Christian Era*, p. 120.

p. 85: "The Sea People fought . . ." Howard, "Philistines," p. 231.

p. 85: "Israel's strength lay . . ." Orlinsky, *Ancient Israel*, p. 57.

p. 86: "The riddle, on its face . . ." Hamlin, *At Risk in the Promised Land: A Commentary on the Book of Judges*, p. 136.

p. 86: "At the beginning of the . . ." Weitzman, "The Samson Story as Border Fiction," p. 170.

p. 89: "It is a lively . . ." Hamlin, *At Risk in the Promised Land: A Commentary on the Book of Judges*, p. 126.

p. 90: "Sow an act . . . " Quoteworld.com, "George Dana Boardman," http://www.quoteworld.org/quotes/1596.

p. 90: "Samson is the muscular . . " George Dana Boardman, "The Story of Samson," *The Old Testament Student* 8, no. 3 (1888): p. 88.

p. 93: "Regarding his qualities . . ." Wiesel, *Wise Men and their Tales: Portraits of Biblical, Talmudic, and Hasidic Masters*, p. 127.

# Glossary

**adversary (noun), adversary (adjective)**—foe; involving antagonistic parties or interests.

**archaeologist (noun), archaeology (noun)**—an archaeologist is a person who specializes in archaeology, the study of past civilizations or cultures by digging up or uncovering the remains of what people made, built, or left behind, and then analyzing the roles these artifacts played in people's lives.

**besiege (verb), siege (noun)**—to surround a fortified place such as a city and attempt to capture it or force it to surrender. Besiegers can try tactics such as cutting off the flow of supplies, attacking the gates or walls, or even deception (the Trojan Horse is an excellent example of the latter tactic).

**circumcision (noun), circumcise (verb), circumcised (adjective)**—to remove the foreskin of the male sexual organ.

**countenance (noun)**—a person's appearance or face.

**covenant (noun)**—an arrangement between two or more people in which they agree to do certain actions or accept certain obligations or responsibilities.

**depredation (noun)**—a laying waste or plundering.

**dowry (noun)**—the property that a woman brings to her spouse in marriage.

**enigma (noun)**—something obscure or hard to understand.

**geology (noun), geologic (adjective)**—the scientific study of the origin, history, and structure of the earth.

**impede (verb)**—to interfere with the progress of.

**incarnate (adjective)**—embodied in flesh; given a bodily, especially a human, form.

**linguistic (adjective), linguistics (noun)**—having to do with language. Linguistics is the study of language.

**monopoly (noun)**—exclusive ownership (as through command of supply); a commodity controlled by one party.

**rout (noun or verb)**—a defeat in which the defeated army falls into complete disorder and its soldiers flee for their lives.

**shalom (interjection)**—used as a Jewish greeting and farewell.

**vassal (noun)**—a person or political entity, such as a city, which is under the control of a more powerful political entity. Often a vassal will be responsible for providing military assistance or paying tribute to his lord.

**wadi (noun)**—a bed or valley of a stream that is dry except in the rainy season, especially in southwestern Asia and northern Africa.

# Further Reading

**BOOKS FOR YOUNG READERS**

Evslin, Bernard. *Signs and Wonders: Tales from the Old Testament*. New York: Four Winds Press, 1981.

Farb, Peter. *The Land, Wildlife, and Peoples of the Bible*. New York: Harper & Row, 1967.

Farrington, Karen. *Historical Atlas of the Holy Lands*. New York: Checkmark Books, 2003.

*The Lion Graphic Bible*. Oxford, England: Lion Publishing, 2001.

Millard, Alan. *Treasures from Bible Times*. Tring, Herts, England: Lion Publishing, 1985.

Motyer, Stephen. *Who's Who in the Bible*. London: DK Publishing, 1998.

Senker, Cath. *Everyday Life in the Bible Lands*. North Mankato, Minn.: Smart Apple Media, 2006.

Van Loon, Hendrik Willem. *The Story of the Bible*. New York: Liveright, 1951.

## BOOKS FOR ADULTS

Beitzel, Barry J. *The Moody Atlas of Bible Lands*. Chicago: Moody Press, 1985.

Bierling, Neal. *Philistines: Giving Goliath His Due*. Marco Polo Monographs. Warren, Pa.: Shangri-La Publications, 2002.

Brettler, Marc Zvi. *The Book of Judges*. London and New York: Routledge, 2002.

Dever, William G. *What Did the Biblical Writers Know and When Did They Know It? What Archaeology Can Tell Us about the Reality of Ancient Israel*. Grand Rapids, Mich.: William B. Eerdmans Publishing, 2001.

Dothan, Trude, and Moshe Dothan. *People of the Sea: The Search for the Philistines*. New York: Macmillan Publishing, 1992.

Grossman, David. *Lion's Honey: The Myth of Samson*. Trans. from the Hebrew by Stuart Schoffman. New York: Canongate, 2006.

King, Philip J., and Lawrence E. Stager. *Life in Biblical Israel*. London: Westminster John Knox Press, 2001.

Rogerson, John. *Atlas of the Bible*. New York: Facts on File Publications, 1985.

# Internet Resources

**http://www.biblical-art.com**

A marvelous Web site with art from ancient to modern times. Artwork can be searched by subject, text, artist, and word.

**http://britishmuseum.org**

At the British Museum's site, visitors can search for Ancient Israel, which will bring up a gallery of photos of artifacts and their histories. There are also links to visit related themes, galleries, cultures, and tours, as well as an excellent online tour of the Middle East.

**http://www.pbs.org/wnet/heritage**

Visitors to this site will find a detailed history of the Jews from their beginnings to modern times. Episode 1, "Beginnings," features interactive presentations and atlases, timelines, and video resources. There is also a page with lesson plans for middle and high school teachers, with abundant resources. This series is also available for purchase as a DVD or video.

**http://www.english.imjnet.org.il**

At this site's home page, go to Galleries and then to Archaeology Wing to view artifacts from the Museum's collections. Introductory texts feature a general introduction to time periods from prehistory to the Islamic period, and include examples of artifacts with explanatory texts and photos that can be enlarged to really show interesting details of each piece.

**http://www.imj.org.il/imagine**

Go to Search Collections and enter the type of artifact you'd like to see (gold, jewelry, pottery, etc.) to bring up photos of examples from the Museum's collections, as well as information that is specific to the artifact or tells how it fit into life in the ancient world. Examples are currently somewhat limited, but the site notes that it is in the pilot stage, and will be expanded.

**http://www.thejewishmuseum.org**

At this site, go first to Collection and Exhibitions, then to Collections Overview for a wide selection of antiquities from the Museum's permanent collection. Each page gives a history of the artifact, and then allows viewers to zoom, pan, and use 3-D features. It's as close as you'll come to actually touching the artifact! There is also a selection of online exhibits.

**http://www.jewishvirtuallibrary.org**

This site offers a comprehensive look at Jewish history from ancient to modern times, and has a number of pages dedicated to archaeology and ancient history. The archaeology page has a huge section on excavation sites, many of which include photos. The text is very readable and offers a wealth of details.

**http://www.people.cornell.edu/pages/bel9/index.html**

Designed as part of a course at Cornell University, this Web site offers a brief but comprehensive introduction to the Philistines as they are seen through the Bible and through the investigations of archaeologists. Each page contains general information on selected topics; page numbers from texts for non-academic audiences are provided, making it easy for readers to further investigate each topic on their own.

**http://www.hope.edu/bandstra/RTOT/RTOT.HTM**
Designed for older students, this Web site features a survey of the Old Testament, with summaries of stories and links to the relevant biblical passages. There is background information as well as photos. Each Study Guide section includes a chapter summary, key terms, and interesting concept questions. This is also available as a hardcover book and CD from Wadsworth/Thomson Learning (some features are available only on the CD).

**http://www.fas.harvard.edu/~semitic**
This Web site from one of the Harvard University museums provides a wealth of well-written and illustrated materials on the ancient Middle East. It includes current online exhibits, an archived one, and looks into the museum's collections and exhibits. Of particular interest is the online exhibit "The Houses of Ancient Israel: Domestic, Royal, Divine," which provides a rich picture of everyday life. Each page begins with a quote from the Bible, followed by very informative and readable text and illustrations or photos.

**http://www.demo.lutherproductions.com/bibletutor**
An excellent general introduction to both the Old and New Testaments, aimed at a young audience, but also useful for adults. It is divided into categories such as Books, People, Dates, and Places; within each category are short but very

clear descriptions and links to other pages in the Tutor, photos, and biblical passages. The Basic Level has free access online, but the Advanced Level must be purchased from Luther Productions (Luther Seminary, St. Paul, Minnesota).

**http://www.museum.upenn.edu/Canaan/index.html**

A wonderful online exhibit about the land of Canaan, with pages detailing the land, economy, religion, and daily life. Each section has a glossary, bibliography, activities designed for children ages eight to twelve, and links to other sites of interest. The activities feature projects for children. If you go to the Museum's home page (http://www.museum.upenn.edu) there are links to other online exhibits, including a spectacular one titled "Treasures from the Royal Tombs of Ur."

# Index

Abdon, 47
Abimelech, 46
Abraham, 7, 8, 11, 21, 23, 26, 48, 50
   and the Angel of the Lord, 51
   and Canaan, 18–20
   and circumcision, 56
   and the Philistines, 81
Ammon, 24, 26
Amos, 9
Amos (Old Testament book), 9
*Ancient Israel* (de Vaux), 56–57, **63**
*Ancient Israel* (Orlinsky), 24
Angel of the Lord, 6, 11, 45, 48,
   50–54, 90
   *See also* angels
angels, 49
Angel of the Lord, 6, 11, 45, 48,
   50–54, 90
   Gabriel, 48, 49
   Michael the Archangel, **45**, 49
Ashdod (city-state), 40, 89
Asherah, 34
Ashkelon (city-state), 40, 63, 66, 89
Ashtoreth, 34, 42, 72
*At Risk in the Promised Land*
   (Hamlin), 80–81, 83, 86

Baal, 34, **42**
Baal-zebub, 72
Barak, 6, **42**, 44, 76
Benjamin, 50

*Biblical History of the Hebrews*
   (Foakes-Jackson), 34, 56, 84085
Bierling, Neal, 37, 38
Boardman, George Dana, 90, 92–93
Book of Judges. *See* Judges (Old
   Testament book)

Caleb, 43
Canaan, **10**, 23–24, 83, 86–87, 89
   and Abraham, 18–20
   conquest of, by Israel, 29–31, **32**,
      44
   division of, among Israel's tribes,
      27–29, 31
   geography of, 24–27, 29
   gods of, **31**, 34, **42**
   religious system in, 30–31, 34
   *See also* Israel; Philistines
Carthage, **36**
Cignani, Carlo, **13**
circumcision, 55–56
covenant of God, 31, 50, 56

Dagon (Philistine god), 72, **74**
David (King), 15, 26, **88**
de Vaux, Roland, 56–57, **63**
Dead Sea, **28**
Deborah, 6, **42**, 44, 76
Delilah, 12, **13**, 14, 69, 71–72, **73**,
   76
DeMille, Cecil B., 12

Numbers in **bold italics** refer to captions.

Deuteronomy (Old Testament book), 8
Documentary Hypothesis, 21
Dothan, Trude and Moshe, 38

Edom, 24
Eglon, *42*, 43
Egypt, 20, *22*, 23, 24, 37–38, 80–81, *82*
Ehud, *42*, 43
Ekron (city-state), 40, 89
Elon, 47
Esau, 56
Exodus (Old Testament book), 21, *22*, 23

Fewell, Danna Nolan, 77–78
Flavius, Josephus, 26, 75
Foakes-Jackson, F. J., 34, 56, 84–85

Gabriel, 48, 49
  *See also* angels
Gath (city-state), 40, 89
Gaza (city-state), 40, 68–69, *70*, 72, 89
Genesis (Old Testament book), 7–8, 20, 21, 26, 50, *53*
giants (Rephaites), 26
Gideon, 6, 45–46
Goliath, 26
Guercino, Giovanni Francesco, *60*

Hamlin, E. John, 80–81, 83, 86
Handel, George Frideric, 13
Heber, 44
"Hebrews." *See* Israel
Howard, David M., Jr., 83–84

Ibzan, 47
Isaac, 8, *19*, 20, 48, 50, 56
  and the Philistines, 81
Isaiah, 9
Isaiah (Old Testament book), 9
Israel
  conquest of Canaan by, 29–31, *32*, 44
  history of, 8–9, 15, 20, 23–24, 27–34, 41–47, 79, 80–85, *91*
  judges of, 6
  and the Midianites, 45–46
  and the Philistines, 6, 12, 15, 16, 39–40, 80–85
  tribes of, 27–29, 31, 34, 40
  *See also* Canaan; Philistines

Jabin (King), 43
Jacob, 8, 20, 50, 51, 56
Jael, 44
Jair, 46
Jephthah, 46–47
Jericho, *32*
  *See also* Joshua
Jesus Christ, 7, 9, 48
*Jewish Literacy* (Telushkin), 12
Job, 8
John the Baptist, 48
Joseph, 8, 20, 50, 56
Joshua, 24, 27, 29–30, 31–33, 41
Joshua (Old Testament book), 27, 29–30, 33
Judges (Old Testament book)
  authorship of, 78
  beginning of, 33–34
  and Delilah, 69, 71
  Israel and the Philistines, 16
  and Israel's history, *91*
  judges in, 11, 42–47
  lion and the honey, *60*
  and prophecy of Samson's birth, 50, 51, 52, 53, 54
  and Samson's birth, 6
  and Samson's destruction of the temple, *74*, 75
  and Samson's feud with the Philistines, 64, 68, 72
  and Samson's legend, 90, 92–93
  and Samson's marriage, 6, 15, 55, 64
  and Samson's mother, 76
  and Samson's riddle, 61–62
  and the tribes of Israel, 40
  *See also* Old Testament

lion, 58, *59*, *60*

Manoah (Samson's father), 48,

50–53, 58, *69*, 75–76
   sacrifice of, 53–54
Mantegna, Andrea, 13, *73*
marriage, 56–57
   of Samson, 6, 15, 55–56, 57–58, 60–64
Mary, 48
McKenzie, John L., 14, 17, 61
Mesopotamia, 18
metalworking, 15, 40, *81*, *84*
Michael the Archangel, *45*, 49
   *See also* angels
Michelangelo, 13, *22*
Midianites, 45–46
Milton, John, 14
mixed marriages, 56–57
   *See also* marriage
Moab, 24, 26, 43
Moses, 21, *22*, 23–24, 31, 43, 51, 56

Nazirites, 6, 11–12, 51, *60*, 71, 80, 89
New Testament, 7, 9, 17
Noah, 8, 21

Old Testament, 51
   Amos, 9
   and childless women, 50
   Deuteronomy, 8
   and the Documentary Hypothesis, 21
   Exodus, 21, *22*, 23
   Genesis, 7–8, 20, 21, 26, 50, *53*
   Isaiah, 9
   Joshua, 27, 29–30, 33
   Proverbs, 8
   Ruth, 78
   *See also* Judges (Old Testament book)
olive orchards, 64, *65*
Orlinsky, Harry M., 24
Othniel, 43

Palestine, 18, *25*, 64
   *See also* Canaan
*People of the Sea* (Dothan), 38
*Peoples of the Old Testament World* (Howard), 83–84

Philistines
   and city-states, 39–40
   gods of, 72
   history of the, 35–40, 80–85
   and Israel, 6, 12, 15, 16, 39–40, 80–85
   Samson's feud with, 12, 15–16, 64–68, 71–72, 74–75, 81, 83
   as "Sea Peoples," 15, 37–38, 85
   *See also* Canaan; Israel
*Philistines: Giving Goliath His Due* (Bierling), 37
popular culture, 12–14, 93
prophecy
   and Samson's birth, 11–12, 48, 50–54
prostitutes, 16, 68–69, 77–78
Proverbs (Old Testament book), 8

Rachel, 50
Ramses III, 38, 81, *82*
Raphael, 49
   *See also* angels
Rebekah, 50
Rembrandt, 13, *62*, *63*
Rephaites (giants), 26
riddle, Samson's, 61–63, 66, 85–86
Rubens, Peter Paul, 13
Ruth (Old Testament book), 78

Saint-Saëns, Camille, 13–14
Samson
   and birth prophecy, 11–12, 48, 50–54
   and Delilah, 12, *13*, 14, 69, 71, 72, *73*, 76
   and the destruction of the temple, 16, 72, 74–75
   feud of, with the Philistines, 12, 15–16, 64–68, 71–72, 74–75, 81, 83
   as a "hero of the faith," 17, 93
   as a judge, 6, *10*, 15, 40, 68, 83, 89
   as legend, 79–80, 85–86, 89–90, 92–93
   and the lion, 58, *59*, *60*
   marriage of, to Philistine, 6, 15, 55–56, 57–58, 60–64

mother of, 11–12, 48, 50–53, 75–76
as a Nazirite, 6, 11–12, 51, **60**, 71, 80, 89
in popular culture, 12–14, 93
and prostitutes, 16, 68–69, 77–78
riddle of, 61–63, 66, 85–86
strength of, 11, 62–63, 71–72, 74–75
and temptations, 6, 17, 89
*See also* Judges (Old Testament book)
*Samson Agonistes* (Milton), 14
*Samson and Delilah* (movie), 12
*Samson et Dalila* (Saint-Saëns), 13–14
*Samson* (Handel), 13
Sarah, 48, 50
Sea Peoples. *See* Philistines
Shamgar, 43
Shimshon. *See* Samson
Sisera, *42*, 43–44
Solomon, 8–9

Telushkin, Joseph, 12, 16
Timnah, 55, 57–58, 63
Tola, 46
Torah, 21
*See also* Old Testament
tribes of Israel, 27–29, 31, 34, 40
*See also* Israel

Ur, 18
Uriel, 49
*See also* angels

van Dyck, Anthony, **76**

wealth
and faith, 7–9
weapons, 15, 40, **81**, **84**
Weitzman, Steve, 57–58, 66
Wiesel, Elie, 79–80, 93
*Wise Men and their Tales* (Wiesel), 79–80
*The World of the Judges* (McKenzie), 14, 61

# Illustration Credits

| | | | |
|---|---|---|---|
| 2: | used under license from Shutterstock, Inc. | | Museum of Art, New York, USA / The Bridgeman Art Library |
| 10: | Scala/Art Resource, NY | 53: | Erich Lessing/Art Resource, NY |
| 13: | Scala/Art Resource, NY | 59: | used under license from Shutterstock, Inc. |
| 14: | © 2009 Jupiterimages Corporation | 60: | Alinari / Art Resource, NY |
| 19: | © 2009 Jupiterimages Corporation | 62: | Erich Lessing/Art Resource, NY |
| 20: | used under license from Shutterstock, Inc. | 63: | Bildarchiv Preussischer Kulturbesitz/Art Resource, NY |
| 22: | used under license from Shutterstock, Inc. | 64: | used under license from Shutterstock, Inc. |
| 23: | used under license from Shutterstock, Inc. | 68: | Scala/Art Resource, NY |
| 25: | used under license from Shutterstock, Inc. | 70: | Scala/Art Resource, NY |
| 27: | used under license from Shutterstock, Inc. | 73: | © 2009 Jupiterimages Corporation |
| | | 74: | © 2009 Jupiterimages Corporation |
| 28: | used under license from Shutterstock, Inc. | 76: | Erich Lessing/Art Resource, NY |
| | | 80: | used under license from Shutterstock, Inc. |
| 31: | Erich Lessing/Art Resource, NY | 82: | used under license from Shutterstock, Inc. |
| 32: | © 2009 Jupiterimages Corporation | | |
| 36: | used under license from Shutterstock, Inc. | 84: | used under license from Shutterstock, Inc. |
| 39: | Erich Lessing/Art Resource, NY | 86: | © 2009 Jupiterimages Corporation |
| 42: | The Art Archive / Bodleian Library, Oxford | 88: | used under license from Shutterstock, Inc. |
| 44: | Scala/Art Resource, NY | 90: | used under license from Shutterstock, Inc. |
| 49: | used under license from Shutterstock, Inc. | 92: | used under license from Shutterstock, Inc. |
| 52: | "The Angel Appearing to Menoah" (oil on canvas), American School / Dahesh | | |

**Cover photo:** "Samson Fighting a Lion" by Clive Uptton (1911-2006). Private Collection/ Look and Learn/ The Bridgeman Art Library

DENISE-RENÉE BARBERET has a doctorate in medieval Spanish literature, and has taught at colleges and universities in Massachusetts for the last twenty years. Her scholarly research has concentrated on depictions of women in medieval texts. She is currently a freelance writer and editor, and prefers to write about the ordinary and the unexpected, which are sometimes not as far apart as one might think. She is also a licensed EMT.